Collection of William Rockhill Nelson Gallery of Art, Kansas City, Missouri.

A Narrative of the Early Days and Remembrances
of Oceola Nikkanochee, Prince of Econchatti

LIBRARY PRESS@UF

AN IMPRINT OF UF PRESS AND
GEORGE A. SMATHERS LIBRARIES

A Narrative of the Early Days and Remembrances of Oceola Nikkanochee, Prince of Econchatti

ANDREW G. WELCH

LibraryPress@UF
GAINESVILLE, FLORIDA

Cover: Map of the West Indies, published in Philadelphia, 1806. From the Caribbean Maps collection in the University of Florida Digital Collections at the George A. Smathers Libraries.

Reissued 2017 by LibraryPress@UF on behalf of the University of Florida
This work is licensed under a Creative Commons Attribution-Noncommercial-No Derivative Works 4.0 Unported License. To view a copy of this license, visit https://creativecommons.org/licenses/by-nc-nd/4.0/. You are free to electronically copy, distribute, and transmit this work if you attribute authorship. Please contact the University Press of Florida (http://upress.ufl.edu) to purchase print editions of the work. You must attribute the work in the manner specified by the author or licensor (but not in any way that suggests that they endorse you or your use of the work). For any reuse or distribution, you must make clear to others the license terms of this work. Any of the above conditions can be waived if you receive permission from the University Press of Florida. Nothing in this license impairs or restricts the author's moral rights.

ISBN 978-1-947372-27-6 (pbk.)
ISBN 978-1-947372-29-0 (ePub)

LibraryPress@UF is an imprint of the University of Florida Press.

| LIBRARY PRESS@UF |

AN IMPRINT OF UF PRESS AND
GEORGE A. SMATHERS LIBRARIES

University of Florida Press
15 Northwest 15th Street
Gainesville, FL 32611-2079
http://upress.ufl.edu

The Florida and the Caribbean
Open Books Series

In 2016, the University Press of Florida, in collaboration with the George A. Smathers Libraries of the University of Florida, received a grant from the National Endowment for the Humanities and the Andrew W. Mellon Foundation, under the Humanities Open Books program, to republish books related to Florida and the Caribbean and to make them freely available through an open access platform. The resulting list of books is the Florida and the Caribbean Open Books Series published by the LibraryPress@UF in collaboration with the University of Florida Press, an imprint of the University Press of Florida. A panel of distinguished scholars has selected the series titles from the UPF list, identified as essential reading for scholars and students.

The series is composed of titles that showcase a long, distinguished history of publishing works of Latin American and Caribbean scholarship that connect through generations and places. The breadth and depth of the list demonstrates Florida's commitment to transnational history and regional studies. Selected reprints include Daniel Brinton's *A Guide-Book of Florida and the South* (1869), Cornelis Goslinga's *The Dutch in the Caribbean and on the Wild Coast, 1580–1680* (1972), and Nelson Blake's *Land into Water—Water into Land* (1980). Also of note are titles from the Bicentennial Floridiana Facsimile Series. The series, published in 1976 in commemoration of America's bicentenary, comprises twenty-five books regarded as "classics," out-of-print works that needed to be in more libraries and readers' bookcases, including Sidney Lanier's *Florida: Its Scenery, Climate, and History* (1875) and Silvia Sunshine's *Petals Plucked from Sunny Climes* (1880).

Today's readers will benefit from having free and open access to these works, as they provide unique perspectives on the historical scholarship on Florida and the Caribbean and serve as a foundation upon which today's researchers can build.

Visit LibraryPress@UF and the Florida and the Caribbean Open Books Series at http://ufdc.ufl.edu/librarypress.

Florida and the Caribbean Open Books Series Project Members

LIBRARY PRESS@UF

Judith C. Russell
Laurie N. Taylor
Brian W. Keith
Chelsea Dinsmore
Haven Hawley

EDITORIAL ADVISORY BOARD

Gary R. Mormino
David C. Colburn
Patrick J. Reakes

UNIVERSITY OF FLORIDA PRESS

Meredith M. Babb
Linda Bathgate
Michele Fiyak-Burkley
Romi Gutierrez
Larry Leshan
Anja Jimenez
Marisol Amador
Valerie Melina
Jane Pollack
Danny Duffy
Nichole Manosh
Erika Stevens

This book is reissued as part of the Humanities Open Books program, funded by a grant from the National Endowment for the Humanities and the Andrew W. Mellon Foundation.

BICENTENNIAL COMMISSION OF FLORIDA.

Governor Reubin O'D. Askew, *Honorary Chairman*
Lieutenant Governor J. H. Williams, *Chairman*
Harold W. Stayman, Jr., *Vice Chairman*
William R. Adams, *Executive Director*

Dick J. Batchelor, Orlando
Johnnie Ruth Clarke, St. Petersburg
A. H. "Gus" Craig, St. Augustine
James J. Gardener, Fort Lauderdale
Jim Glisson, Tavares
Mattox Hair, Jacksonville
Thomas L. Hazouri, Jacksonville
Ney C. Landrum, Tallahassee
Mrs. Raymond Mason, Jacksonville
Carl C. Mertins, Jr., Pensacola
Charles E. Perry, Miami
W. E. Potter, Orlando
F. Blair Reeves, Gainesville
Richard R. Renick, Coral Gables
Jane W. Robinson, Cocoa
Mrs. Robert L. Shevin, Tallahassee
Don Shoemaker, Miami
Mary L. Singleton, Jacksonville
Bruce A. Smathers, Tallahassee
Alan Trask, Fort Meade

vi   BICENTENNIAL COMMISSION.

Edward J. Trombetta, Tallahassee
Ralph D. Turlington, Tallahassee
William S. Turnbull, Orlando
Robert Williams, Tallahassee
Lori Wilson, Merritt Island

GENERAL EDITOR'S PREFACE.

OF the many interesting and richly colorful personalities who have moved across the Florida stage at one time or another during its nearly 500 years of recorded history, few are so intriguing and yet so mystifying as Dr. Andrew Welch, the English physician who befriended a young Indian boy in the Florida wilderness, and became an outcast from society because of his kindness. Welch is the author of the three *Narratives* which have been edited by Frank Laumer for the Bicentennial Floridiana Facsimile Series. They are *A Narrative of the Early Days and Remembrances of Oceola Nikkanochee,* *A Narrative of the Life and Sufferings of Mrs. Jane Johns,* and *A Narrative of the Life of Benjamin Benson.*

Through careful research, Mr. Laumer has brought to light many interesting biographical details of Welch's early life, as conflicting as some of this information seems to be. Born in Nazeing,

Essex, England, he studied medicine and practiced this profession in London. It is known that he was married at least twice, that he was the father of several children, and that he was "a most successful general practitioner." But even these basic facts are somewhat beclouded in mystery, and if there are contradictions and questions over even the basics of Welch's life, there is even more puzzlement about some of his later activities. In 1840, Welch described his delight in returning to England "after an absence of twenty years." Yet, the records, as Laumer has examined them, indicate that he was actually present in England some, if not all, of this time. He did indeed travel to foreign lands, perhaps to Bermuda, the West Indies, and to the United States.

In 1838, Dr. Welch was in Florida, and there he began a series of adventures that might have been concocted by a writer of fantasy and fiction. Florida was still a territory when he arrived with his family to live and practice medicine in Jacksonville. It was a time of danger and trouble for all Floridians. After years of harassment and oppression, the Florida Seminoles were desperately resisting an effort to uproot them from their traditional homes and force their removal to lands west of the Mississippi. The Second Seminole War, which began in 1835, would be the longest and bloodiest Indian conflict in American history. Many tragedies were suffered by both sides. In one attack on a settlement near Jacksonville, Mrs. Jane

Johns was scalped, and Dr. Welch was called in to tend her wounds. A *Narrative of the Life and Sufferings of Mrs. Jane Johns*, first published in 1837, and now being republished in this facsimile volume, is one of the fascinating frontier documents emerging from this period of American history. Dr. Welch not only treated Mrs. Johns, but he and his wife accompanied the afflicted lady on a journey to Savannah and to Charleston. It was claimed that Mrs. Johns received visits from curious persons who listened to her sad tale, examined her wounds, and offered her donations of money. Dr. Welch's role in this affair is not quite clear. There were those who accused him of being unscrupulous and of promoting Mrs. John's affliction, yet there is no evidence revealing any personal gain that he received from this adventure.

Even more intriguing is the relationship that developed between Dr. Welch and a young Seminole boy of five or six years, who was brought into Jacksonville as a captive of war. His name was Nikkanochee. In time, he became a family ward, and Dr. Welch assumed the responsibility for Nikkanochee's care, protection, and education. When the Welch family returned to England in 1840, Oceola Nikkanochee began a new life there. *A Narrative of the Early Days and Remembrances of Oceola Nikkanochee* was one of the three books authored by Dr. Welch which are now being republished.

The third book, *A Narrative of the Life of Ben-*

jamin Benson, is the tale of a black man whom Dr. Welch encountered on the streets of Worcester, England. The story of Benson's life is as fascinating as that of Dr. Welch's. Born a slave, he gained his freedom, but was re-enslaved when he returned to America. He then escaped by stowing away on a ship bound for Nassau, and finally reached England. The black man and the doctor became friends, and Welch told his story in the third of his narratives.

His experiences with a lady who was attacked and scalped by a band of marauding Indians on the Florida frontier, his affection for a young Seminole Indian refugee, and his friendship with a former black slave reveal the breadth of Andrew Welch's interest in people as human beings, regardless of how the rest of society regarded them. Dr. Welch seemed willing to become an outcast himself in order to support the principles to which he had dedicated his life. His *Narratives* reveal him to be a gentle, humane, and kind man. One is also able to perceive from his writing insight and interpretation of Florida people and Florida scenes not readily available in other contemporary books and manuscripts.

The American Revolution Bicentennial Commission of Florida, from the time of creation sought to reflect on Florida's rich and exciting past, which reaches back to the sixteenth century when white Europeans first made contact with the Indians living along the state's eastern shores. The Commission developed a major Bicentennial publications program, which included the reprinting of twenty-five rare volumes on Florida history. The Welch *Narratives* make up one of the volumes in the Bicentennial Floridiana Facsimile Series. Each facsimile volume is being edited by a recognized scholar such as Frank Laumer. An interpretive essay accompanies each introduction and an index has been compiled.

Frank Laumer is a land developer living north of Dade City, Florida. A native of New York, he has lived in Florida since 1937. He is a past director of the Florida Historical Society, and a former member of the editorial board of the *Florida Historical Quarterly*. He has contributed articles to that and other scholarly and professional journals. His book, *Massacre!*, describes the Indian attack on Major Francis L. Dade and his company in 1835. It was published by the University of Florida Press.

The editor and publisher thank the Library of Congress for making possible the reproduction of its copy of the Benson narrative.

SAMUEL PROCTOR
General Editor of the
BICENTENNIAL FLORIDIANA
FACSIMILE SERIES.

University of Florida.

INTRODUCTION.

———◆———

IT is a presumption for any man to deal with another's life, whether the subject still be in the course of his years or if he has gone to whatever, if anything, awaits him. Our understanding of ourselves, with whom we spend a lifetime, is so incomplete, really such a mixture of guesswork and hope, that it ill qualifies us to appraise, to evaluate another. Yet we try. Perhaps it is in the hope that in trying to find the essence of someone else we shall stumble on some new comprehension of ourselves. Whether our quarry be "doctor, lawyer, Indian chief," it can be assumed that he, too, attempted to manipulate his days toward these goals created in the tissue of his soul which must have beckoned him erratically but unceasingly onward until drive and life came to an end. Did he indeed have these goals? Perhaps again it is a safe assumption that if he did not have them we would not be in search of him for those who made no search are not likely to be sought. Then did he reach them? Did he ever know that moment, however brief, when his fingers brushed the source? And what did it mean to him? What did it cost him?

The search for another is assuredly a paper trail, a veritable scavenger hunt; an old laundry ticket, a letter to a friend, statistics of a life, a book he read, or better a book he wrote. In the case of James Andrew Welch, M.D., member of the Royal College of Surgeons, licentiate of the Apothecaries Hall, there are three books: *A Narrative of the Life and Sufferings of Mrs. Jane Johns, A Narrative of the Early Days and Remembrances of Oceola Nikkanochee* and *A Narrative of the Life of Benjamin Benson.*[1]

Andrew Welch—as he was referred to in his lifetime—was born in Nazeing, Essex, England, on March 20, 1797.[2] The Welch families were sizable landowners and farmers in the north of the parish, though the principal yield seems to have been children. James Andrew was the tenth child of seventeen born to William and Mary Welch.[3] Nothing is known of his childhood or how he made it through the fraught days of youth. The first real glimpse of him is as a young man of twenty-one, admitted to the College of Surgeons in London on April 3, 1818. In August of that year, perhaps with the tentative security of his medical degree, he established residence in Kingsland Place (Road) in the parish of St. Leonard, county of

Middlesex, Shoreditch, a suburb in the northeastern part of London.[4] This was the area with which his life and practice would be principally associated. On May 8, 1819, Welch married Jane Gliddon, a girl from Chipping Onger, a village nine miles from Nazeing.[5] The inference seems that with a profession and a household, Welch had brought his childhood sweetheart to the city. Nine months later, their first child Jane Welch was born.[6] The young family shared Welch's professional advancement as licentiate of the Apothecaries Hall in 1821, which enabled him to prepare and sell drugs. In 1822, Henry James Wordsworth Welch was born.[7] A third child, Emily Welch, was born in October 1824, and died almost immediately.[8]

And so it went. A wife, a home, children, "a most successful general practitioner."[9] Or did it? Later, in 1840, Welch wrote, "I rejoiced to find myself once more [in England]—after an absence of twenty years."[10] Should one assume that he left England around 1820? An apothecary's license was not likely granted to someone not in the country for two decades. And the children? Conceived and born to an absentee father? Perhaps "twenty years" was an exaggeration, yet in *Benjamin Benson*, Welch wrote: "having resided *many years* in the countries where the principal scenes of this narrative have been enacted."[11] The tax rolls show that through September 1833 taxes were paid in his name on property in London, except for the two-year period, March 1828–March 1830, where *xvi*   INTRODUCTION.

his quarters were listed by the collector "empty" or under another occupant. Are these, in fact, the years spent "in the countries [Bermuda, the Bahama Islands, the United States, and Canada] where the principal scenes of this narrative have been enacted"? The text seems to rule out Canada, leaving a real possibility that he may have taken his family to Bermuda, the West Indies, and the United States. If he was ever in this area of the world at all, and there is reason to believe that he was, it must have been at this time. If so, why did he go? For a young man already established in his practice, with a wife and two children, to pull up stakes and take ship for the West Indies, the inducement must have been strong, the goal clear. Perhaps it was a necessity because of the health of the family. Tuberculosis had settled in the city with the soot and the sewage; the lure of new land and fresh air may have played their part. If health had been the reason, the voyage proved to be a reprieve, not a pardon. It is a possibility that Jane was frail, and she may have died in those lands away from home.

In July 1838, Welch was in Florida where he purchased land "in trust for [Frances] Mary Ann, wife of Andrew."[12] Since divorce was rare, it can be assumed that Jane had died in the interim, though the parish records which list the births, marriages, and deaths of the Welch family make no mention of this as having occurred in London. Whether with Jane still living or whether as a

INTRODUCTION.

widower, Welch returned to London in 1830 from his first trip abroad. It was after this time that it seems likely that he married Frances Ann Clark, the lady who would share his Florida adventure and outlive him by twenty years.[13] Now begins a strange, inexplicable decade in the doctor's life. His lifeline seems to split, almost as though from this time on he leads two lives, one in England and another in Florida. His imprint is on each. Because Florida is the theme, while Andrew Welch is our only subject, we will follow him first to Florida.

The St. Johns County Court records list him as defendant in a case of trespass, September 15, 1832.[14] James Gould, editor of the St. Augustine newspaper, wrote two years later: "Some years ago, say ten or twelve, Welsh [sic] came to St. Augustine."[15] Welch in 1832 was thirty-five, and his ten-year old son may have been with him, as well as a nephew, Gesborne.[16] He was probably motivated more by a vast curiosity about this raw, new country than by economic or humanitarian impulses. All but the land was new. Beyond the docks at Jacksonville there was hardly more than a store and an inn, a few scattered houses and farms, the American flag, slavery, and Seminole Indians. A more startling change from the lowering skies, the ancient charms, the filth of London could hardly be imagined. And startling too must have been his first sight of the "noble savage." Raised in the European tradition that still debated whether the American Indians were descended from the lost tribes of Israel, that pictured them as living carefree lives in an Eden-like land, his first view of Seminole rejects who hung about the fringes of white settlements must have seemed an unhappy reality. It was not. The real destruction of the Seminoles, social and biological, had not yet begun, though the infectious bite of western civilization had consumed the heart of more than twenty Indian nations along the eastern seaboard from Canada south through Georgia. The United States, so recently "conceived in liberty and dedicated to the proposition that all men are created equal" had continued the crusade—disease, deportation, and death—begun by their English, French, Dutch and Spanish progenitors. The Seminole, thus far spared by a geographical reprieve and ignored by a Spanish landlord who was suffering a mortal illness of his own, had lived on in forest and meadow, along the streams, as much a part of his environment as bird or tree or bear, and quite as unable to conceive of *ownership* of the earth.

When Florida became part of the American Union in 1821, new rules applied. American settlers, always land hungry, were moving into the new territory from Georgia and the Carolinas. There was no room for Indians. The agreement between the Seminoles and the Spanish in 1784 which had guaranteed Indian title to the land was not considered binding on the new owners. The diplomatic tools of intimidation and bribery effected a new agreement, the Treaty of Moultrie Creek in 1823. The Seminoles were to abandon all coastal lands east and west, all of northern Florida and everything south of Lake Okeechobee. The corridor allowed them was a "wasteland of shallow lakes, sluggish rivers and undrained swamps incapable of productive cultivation," described at the time by a white man, as "by far the poorest and most miserable region I ever beheld."[17] The President signed this agreement and the Congress approved the guarantee that here the Seminoles would finally be left alone; white men were forbidden to cross the paper line.

Andrew Welch, according to Gould, "made his debut [in Florida] in a lecture on *diet* in which he attempted to show the sin of using as food, anything having life." "The lecture," Gould noted, "excited but little attention, nor did the lecturer acquire the reputation of a Solomon, and after a few days he retired to the region of the beautiful St. John's, about the meanderings of which stream he continued to meander for some years, seeking a livelihood in such ways as accidental circumstances should place before him."[18]

Gould admitted to knowing little about Welch; he never "thought him of sufficient consequence to desire his acquaintance; but little men, and bad men, may sometimes by their impudence and effrontery, and fraud, do much injury. So it happens with Welsh." According to Gould, "Soon after the celebrated lecture just noticed, he [Welch] began as we are informed, to acquire a taste for the good things in life, and indicated a willingness to gratify that taste whenever it could be done at the expense of his neighbors and friends. Not gaining confidence as a practitioner of Medicine, he adopted various schemes to maintain himself. At one time he made discovery of a lime stone quarry and applied to our legislature for an exclusive privilige to quarry stone."[19] While one searches for the man, regardless of his qualities, it would be difficult not to discern a bias on the part of Mr. Gould. A bias that becomes more understandable when we recall that Gould was writing in a southern community in 1843, when Welch had begun speaking out against slavery. The matter which caused Gould and other Floridians consternation concerned the attack and scalping of a white woman, Mrs. Johns, near Jacksonville by marauding Indians. Allegedly Welch had used the tragic incident to exploit Mrs. Johns for his own interest. If true, it proved, as Gould believed, that Welch was self-centered and ruthless.

According to Gould, "It was a great day for him [Welch] when the Indians made a descent upon the settlement of [Jane and Clement] John's [sic] near Jacksonville. If Mrs. John's had not lost her scalp on that occasion Welsh would still, in all probability, have been prowling around in Florida for his prey. But she lost her scalp; and he being benevolently inclined became her attending physician."[20] The *Jacksonville Courier* reported: "Dr. Welch readily volunteered his services as physician. This is the more creditable to Dr. Welch as he was then the only physician in town."[21] As Welch himself described the matter in his journal, "On Saturday, September 17, 1836, I was requested by a committee, formed of the most respectable inhabitants of this city (Jacksonville) to visit Mrs. Johns, who, it was reported on good authority, had recently been dangerously wounded and scalped by Indians. I immediately complied."[22]

Welch's journal and it's accompanying text, *A Narrative of the Life and Sufferings of Jane Johns*, published "Exclusively For Her Benefit" in 1837, was his first literary effort. With his two later publications, it forms a kind of three-stage development in viewpoint. In this *Narrative* Welch seemed to view events with the myopic vision of a participant. Among so-called "frontier documents" the *Narrative* is mild enough, though one looks in vain for any attempt by Welch to view this tragic episode as incidental to the overall conflict, a virtual duel to the death by two alien cultures. Contemporary English military journals "were inclined to treat it [the conflict] as a rather objectionable affair between unspeakable Americans and poor downtrodden Indians."[23] To Welch, however, at this time, the Seminoles were "merciless savages," "barbarous enemies," "brutal foes," "murderous villains," "hell hounds," "monsters." Direct involvement with the victims of war is likely to produce a different reaction than a theory of that war developed 3,000 miles away.

Some two weeks before Welch's services were called upon in behalf of Mrs. Johns, Colonel John Warren, head of the Florida Militia, an Englishman who made his home in Jacksonville, had brought to the city a war captive, a Seminole boy of five or six years, who gave his name as Nikkanochee. Warren's concern for the child had prompted him to bring him into his own household, first in Jacksonville, and then, when Warren, his wife, and children moved to their country residence, they took the Indian boy along. He lived with the family for a year. The Welch and Warren families seem to have been friendly, a likely circumstance since there were few people of education in the little settlement of Jacksonville at that time.

For Welch the months from the summer of 1836 through autumn of the following year must have been disturbing. Caught up as he was in the passions of his time and place, he seems to have been still capable of independent thought. Though he had mended flesh torn by Indians, the coming of Nikkanochee seems to have brought him to a personal, physical confrontation with the American answer to "the Indian question." It is one thing to condemn a stranger to death and quite another to watch him die. "Merciless savages, barbarous enemies" had shot and scalped Jane Johns and many another, but this was a human being, a child, lost and alone. Beneath the dusky skin was there a different heart? Behind the dark wondering eyes were there not the same vast ignorance and wisdom of every child? Was it possible to hate this boy, to kill him? And if not him, then how his people? Were they not men?

Dr. Welch continued to administer "kindness, care and unceasing attention" to Mrs. Johns through the next four months of her recovery. Newspapers had brought details of her condition to the attention of the people of Charleston, and they asked that she come to that city for what can only be considered a morbid interest in viewing a scalpless woman. It was implied that the civic hat of Charleston might be passed for her benefit. With this in mind, ten "distinguished gentlemen" of Jacksonville urged that Welch travel with the invalid to Charleston via Savannah.

Gould, the skeptic, reported: "he [Welch] went north with her, with more advantage to himself than benefit to her; but true it is that Mrs. John's returned to Florida, a poor woman, though considerable sums of money went into the hands of Welch for her benefit."[24] Gould's premise that any funds raised went to Welch seems to be invalid unless Welch was able to hoodwink and/or enlist the aid of a good many respectable citizens, not only in Jacksonville, but also in Savannah and Charleston.

On February 16, 1837, Dr. Welch, with Mrs. Welch and Mrs. Johns, arrived in Savannah.[25]

After depositing the ladies at the Mansion House, Welch, with manuscript in hand, dropped in on the editor of the *Savannah Daily Georgian*. Within hours his story was in print: "Our readers remember the particulars of the attack by a party of . . . Indians in September last, upon . . . Mrs. Johns. . . . Mrs. Johns is now on her way on a visit to Charleston, in company with her humane surgeon, Dr. Adam [sic] Welch, who was one of a gallant little band . . . who . . . hastened . . . to her relief, and escorted her to . . . Jacksonville. The condition of Mrs. Johns, (her wound of five months not yet healed, and requiring the attention of her surgeon) presents a strong appeal to the sympathies of our citizens. . . . The narrative of her sufferings . . . has been submitted to our perusal, and cold must that heart be, which would not beat to avenge the wrongs of this helpless woman. . . . Mrs. Johns has taken lodgings, while in the city, at the Mansion House, where we learn, she will be able to receive the visits of our citizens, particularly the ladies. . . . Her narrative . . . when detailed in her own language . . . cannot fail to excite additional sympathy.

"We are authorized to state that all contributions for her relief will be received between twelve, A.M. and two o'clock P.M. of every day this week by Rev. Edward Neufville, at the Pulaski House."[26]

Four days later, Welch had enlisted the aid of seven additional clergymen and a Mrs. Douvilles to accept donations, and those citizens who paid visits to the sufferer were encouraged to contribute at the Mansion House itself where compassion might more directly touch the purse. "Dr. Welch respectfully invites his professional brethren, to attend at the time of dressing the head of Mrs. Johns, say 10 A.M."[27]

The party sailed from Savannah, arriving March 2, in Charleston, aboard the steam packet *William Seabrook*.[28] At this time Charleston was a major port of embarkation for the volunteer soldiers who were answering the cries for help from settlers and slave hunters within the Florida territory. In such a place, in such a time, there was room for only one opinion with regard to Indians. The Seminole devastation of Francis Dade's command, December 1835, as he invaded their land, had brought rallying cries from his fellow officers; their bodies "lie bleaching in the air defaced by Negroes and torn by obscene birds— Rouse up Florida! . . . and let us now think of nothing but vengeance."[29] Sensible enough, if reasoning is optional. And all around Andrew Welch were the horrified witnesses to the tragedy of Jane Johns; the patriotic speeches, the grand balls, the throbbing bands that were sending young men out of the harbor, past Fort Sumter so recently ceded to the federal government, and off to war.[30]

For a month and more the show went on in Charleston. The sight of Mrs. Johns' skull, "divested of its natural integuments . . . from the upper part of the forehead (leaving at its commencement only a few hairs) to the occiput, nine inches and a half—from above one ear to the opposite, nine inches," should have convinced even those with the strongest doubts.[31] Then on April 15, 1837, the party began its journey home, first to Savannah on the schooner *Exit*, and then on to Florida.[32]

Welch seems to have become strongly drawn toward Nikkanochee who, with Colonel Warren's family, had also come back to Jacksonville. Perhaps the visit to Charleston with its peculiar implications had strengthened his interest in the Indian lad. "My sympathies for the little captive became daily more strongly excited; as I fancied I observed in him the dawning of the good qualities peculiar to his race; and reflected, that notwithstanding the kind of treatment he now received, he would eventually be claimed as a prisoner of war, and undergo the fate which many of his exiled tribe had already suffered."[33]

In June 1837 Welch purchased the first of several tracts of land south of the St. Johns River and some twelve miles east of Jacksonville.[34] He and his family continued to live in town, but his principal efforts were now directed toward the development of his property which he was to call "the new town of St. Johns."[35] For the next year he continued adding to his holdings for a total of more than 1,000 acres bounded on the north by the river.

Welch's interest in Nikkanochee, whom he saw

regularly, continued. The boy was treated like a member of the Warren family, eating, playing, and sleeping with the other children. At his capture, the boy had been emaciated, but under the care and interest of Colonel and Mrs. Warren, he had regained his strength and energy. He had also acquired a fair command of English, and was able to communicate with the other children. He was reticent with adults, however, never giving his own name or the names of his own family. Welch noted: "his fear of strangers was very great, and of the white country people, or *Crackers*, as they are . . . called, he had a particular dread. . . . His peculiar situation at length determined me, if possible, to constitute myself his guardian; and Colonel Warren being on the point of making an important change in his own family, gave me an opportunity of preferring my request: it was willingly granted, and this friendless child accordingly came under my immediate protection on the 31st of October 1837."[36]

Earlier, in January 1837, when Dr. Welch had been asked by the Jacksonville residents to accompany Mrs. Johns to Charleston, they had regarded him warmly, as is clear from their letter: "We . . . tender you our expression of admiration of your unwearied and kind attention in the exercise of your noble profession since you have dwelt among us; the exalted stand you have taken in Florida as a surgeon, and the urbanity of your deportment as a gentleman, claim our warmest sympathies."[37] Succoring a white woman was one thing; adopting an Indian child was something else. That was definitely not a part of the accepted code.

But unlike most men who stand in a fair way of achieving both professional and business success, Andrew Welch seems not to have cut himself loose from thought and concern and meaning. Those deeper values about which man creates religion, writes poetry, and weaves philosophical ideals were brought to the surface rather than submerged by the modest wealth and fame that he had achieved. He has made it clear that his interest in a non-white brought upon him the hostility of those people among whom he had dwelt.

In January 1838, Welch acquired a second property, 800 acres of riverfront. There was a "commodious family house" already on the land, and to this "estate," Welch soon moved his family, including Nikkanochee. It could not have been an easy thing for Welch to uproot his life, to start again in what was quite literally a new field. Jacksonville had been no metropolis, but this new home was close to being a wilderness. Gone was the "eminently successful" practice, the position of post surgeon, and whatever may have existed in the way of social amenities. It is doubtful that Welch moved away from Jacksonville entirely because of a sudden interest in land development. And now, if not before, his growing opposition to

INTRODUCTION. xxix

the destruction of the Seminoles also included human slavery. Separated from his former Jacksonville associates, and alone with his family, Nikkanochee, and whatever farm and house workers there were, there was still much time left for reflection. Welch was an intelligent and educated man. He had come to America in a time of burgeoning freedoms throughout the western world. He had thrown in his knowledge and his youth with the pioneers of young America. Although he was now a middleaged man, his mind was young; he had insisted upon his right to an unpopular idea. Alone now, partially because of that idea, other ideas would be born.

Welch was determined to protect and help Nikkanochee as best he could. Not content with simply providing for the security of the child, he had come to enjoy his company as time and proximity broke down the barriers. Earlier in Jacksonville the boy had attended "a school with the children of several respectable families in the neighbourhood, kept by a lady of conciliatory manners and superior understanding."[38] In the woods along the St. Johns River, however, "he had full opportunities of indulging his taste for the wilder accomplishments of hunting and fishing."[39] Welch watched the physical and mental development of the boy, through these, his seventh and eighth years. He learned as much of the boy's earlier life as Nikkanochee could recall, while their mutual education continued, and affection, at least on the part of the doctor, seems to have grown to paternal depth.

When he first moved to his property at St. Johns, he undertook to open a "road of communication to St. Augustine, upwards of forty miles."[40] Taking the boy with him, he lived a month in the woods with a dozen slaves hired from their owners to clear the road south to St. Augustine. From an "interesting" child, Nikkanochee had by degrees become "ward," "protegee," " my little friend," "my boy," and finally "I . . . determined to adopt and cherish him as my own child."[41] Welch describes one scene with less effulgence and with somewhat more restraint than usual, when he was camped one night with Nikkanochee and the blacks. Considering his own position and the condition of the child and the men, it is apparent why "Nothing can ever efface [the scene] from my memory. . . . We were . . . in a part of the forest that had not been visited by as many white people since the country was owned by the Spaniards. Throughout the universe, a wilder spot could not be selected. . . . There were three very large fires made of the resinous pine logs, which threw up a glare of light, that gave to the dense woods in our rear a shade as dark as Erebus. About ten o'clock the full broad moon threw up her silvery beams through the tall stately pines which sighed mournfully to the breeze.—Save this melancholy sound, with the dismal hooping of the owl—with, now and then the howling wolves at a distance—all was still, desolate, and dreary.

"At this solemn moment, I reflected upon the condition of the slaves by whom I was surrounded. —'Tis true they were then happy—as they were the whole time while in my employ—I knew that this contentment was solely a relative feeling; a negro always comforts himself with having got rid of the past—he seldom reflects upon the future; if there be ever so small a chance of temporary happiness, he readily embraces it without embittering the moment by gloomy forebodings. They did not hear the crack of the 'Drivers'' whip, and they were happy. Under an impression that I might in some measure benefit them by wholesome admonition, and comfort them by prayer, I ordered them into the open space in the centre of the camp fires, and forming them into a circle, I placed the young Indian on his knees, and desired him to repeat *The Lord's Prayer*. No sooner had he raised his little plaintive voice to Heaven, than the negroes followed his example with fervour and devotion. Here was a scene that might have softened the heart of the most obdurate sceptic—the sight of this young savage in his native wilds, offering up his orisons to Almighty God, accompanied by slaves even less informed than himself upon the attributes of prayer—with the solemn stillness of the wilderness, combined to make this the most impressive scene I had ever witnessed.

"The prayer ended, I addressed them upon the peculiarity of their position in the human family; and endeavoured to ameliorate their condition by pouring a balm into the iron galls of slavery. I pointed out to them the necessity of obedience to their masters, and to depend upon their own worthiness for comfort and happiness. I assured them (and with truth) that their wants were fewer than many others of the human race—and, although not by the hand of kindness, they were supplied with all that was absolutely requisite for their subsistence—that it was to the interest of their proprietors to keep them in health, for their profits depended upon the negroes' physical strength. I advised them to rely upon a just God; and assured them that, by maintaining a virtuous and good life, one day they would find their reward."[42]

By August 1838 Welch had so far progressed with his land development that he ran the first of several advertisements in the St. Augustine paper.[43] From the evidence of deeds in the county records, Welch seems to have had a steady, although not a sensational, success with his town of St. Johns. General Peter Sken Smith had become a "joint proprietor," and countless documents were signed under his name for a decade and more.

That concern for the well-being of Nikkanochee was increasingly on his mind is evident. Virtually cut off from his medical practice by the comparative isolation of his property, seemingly ostracized by those who had so recently praised him,

INTRODUCTION.　　　*xxxiii*

he suffered from "the jealousy and undisguised hostility of my white neighbours." Continuing apprehensive for Nikkanochee's safety, "we sought for him a secure retreat in the dense woods ... to which we instructed him to retire on the least warning of danger. The approach of a steam-boat on the river, or the landing of strangers, roused our anxiety, when we would despatch him to his place of concealment, with instructions to remain until he heard our preconcerted signal."[44] These were hardly ideal conditions for living a normal life, yet for two years the Welches remained, developing their land and remaining isolated from their neighbors. "Finding I was educating him, [they] became alarmed lest he might hereafter become dangerous amongst the tribes, and insisted on his being sent with the rest of the captives into the interior of the country. ... Among the whites in Florida it was evident that my protection would not long prove his safeguard; and most ardently did I long for the security and freedom of 'my native land'."[45]

The move to St. Johns was only a pause on the way home. Perhaps Welch had thought that the ill-feeling created by his sheltering of the Indian boy would fade with time and distance, but if so, the estrangement was all the more discouraging. What had been a possibility all along finally became a certainty in 1840. "My determination to embark for England with my young charge, was soon fixed, and almost as soon executed; and I joyfully left this blood-stained country on Thursday, the 28th of May, 1840."[46] He traveled first to Savannah where the party changed ships and where "the Captain assured me that he ran considerable risk in receiving him on board."[47] After a month at sea, however, Welch, his family, and Nikkanochee docked safely in Liverpool. Nikkanochee "was now (it may truly be said,) in the land of freedom; where I rejoiced to find myself once more—after an absence of twenty years."[48]

Twenty years? He left England in 1820? Then who is the Andrew Welch whose three children's birth records are duly noted in the parish register for 1820, 1822, and 1824? Two of the children died, and their burials took place in 1824 and 1831. All the records list the home address of Welch as Kingsland Road which is incontestably that of *our* Andrew Welch. James Andrew Welch, M.D. paid taxes on the property at this address, not only for the years previously indicated as his residence, but as late as September 1833, one year after his involvement in a trespess suit in Florida. Are there two Dr. Welchs, both living at the same address, or did one Dr. Welch sail back and forth across the Atlantic almost like a week-end commuter?[49] Could someone else have paid the taxes for him and signed his name? Perhaps he *was* there for the birth and death of his children, and meant to write, "after an absence of *ten* years." Maybe. But what about the *Treatise on Tinea Capitis*? The author is J. A. Welch, Member of the Royal College of Surgeons, and Licenciate of The

Apothecaries Hall. This volume is a sixty-three page "Classification of the Forms Under Which It [Tinea Capitis] Manifests Itself, a Brief Analysis of the Theory of Inflamation and Infection and a Description of A MEDICATED STEAM BATH, Invented by The Author, For the Treatment and Cure of Diseases of the Scalp." The author states in the preface, "I have been at considerable expense in procuring drawings from life, illustrative of the different forms and stages of Ringworm; accurate plates, engraved from them, are . . . in the text." In all, a work of some depth. This preface is dated September 1837, and the address is Terrace, Dalton. Dr. Welch includes an extract from his notebook giving the progress of a patient under his care for the period April 24–May 8, 1837. In a footnote to this case, he describes his own accidental inoculation with the disease and ensuing symptoms from which he did not recover for three weeks, or until the middle of May. Yet on April 15, as has been noted, *someone* named Andrew Welch was returning to Savannah, Georgia, from Charleston, and in June purchased land in Florida.

A last curiosity anent these parallel lives. Referring to the volume *Tinea Capitis*, the author states "my first humble effort at authorship," though seven months earlier, February 4, 1837, he had dedicated Jane Johns' *Narrative*, and shortly afterward had taken it to Charleston for publication.[50]

And so the decade of Welch's American adventure ended. With his wife, his surviving son, and Nikkanochee, he returned to London and to the old address, and once again he took up his medical practice.[51] It has never been inexpensive to travel across the Atlantic, and large profits are rarely earned by abruptly leaving your business in the hands of a substitute. To build up a neglected practice takes time and in the meanwhile Nikkanochee needed a basic education. For eighteen months Welch maintained him within his own household, "his chief amusement [being] to visit Mr. [George] Catlin's exhibition at the Egyptian Hall."[52] Nikkanochee's own portrait was soon to hang among the many American Indians already there. Another artist, Frank A. Wilkin, also painted Nikkanochee's portrait, and it was exhibited at the Royal Academy, Trafalgar Square.[53] Both paintings show him in native dress, the Catlin in more or less everyday clothing, and the one by Wilkin in more formal, if somewhat fanciful, costume. A playmate later wrote: "I once saw him in his native dress and the only thing that I can remember was that he wore a cap surrounded by a wreath of hummingbirds."[54]

In addition to the portraits, "A very correct cast of this child's head was taken by Mr. Donovan, *Principal of the London Phrenological Institution.* . . . Mr. Donovan has discovered a mode of taking casts by which the oppressive impediment to breathing during the operation is entirely obviated." Mr. Donovan, according to a contemporary, devoted "his entire time to the practice and teaching of phrenology," as well as to selling casts of heads at three shillings sixpence each.[55] The whereabouts of this cast of Nikkanochee's, if it still exists, is unknown. H. C. Donovan, son of the phrenologist, wrote in 1913, "when my father left London for America in 1854, his collections of casts, skulls etc was dispersed. On his resuming his practice in London in 1857, he was able to regain possession of some of these. I was too young to remember much about the first collection but I never heard the cast of the red Indian youth ever spoken of."[56]

Before emigrating to America a decade earlier, Welch had established a friendship with the Reverend James Sherman. Mr. Sherman and his wife, though they had children of their own, took a strong and kindly interest in the Indian boy. "At length, after much consultation with her husband . . . it was determined to receive him into her house and to adopt and educate him as her child. . . . Many blamed her for incurring so great a risk, taking a half-civilized boy into the family."[57]

Both health and finances seem to have had a part in Welch's allowing the Shermans to care for the boy. He had, moreover, achieved his goal, "having wrested one so amiable and helpless from ignorance, famine, toil, and wretchedness" if not "to become . . . in future years, an ornament to civilized society, and a useful member in the community of intellectual life."[58]

Andrew Welch having achieved the first stage of his goal for Nikkanochee, the Reverend Mr. Sherman set about achieving the second. In January 1842 the boy was enrolled in the Mill Hill Grammar School, located "in the countryside north of London which over its comparatively short period of existence, had made something of a name for itself. In spite of its imposing building with its portico overlooking the wide valley to Harrow, it was not a big school—there were only seventy-eight pupils . . . having been opened in a nearby house some thirty-five years earlier by a group of protestant dissenters. . . . Their experience had ensured . . . more liberal attitudes to life and religion generally."[59] It is difficult to imagine that the wildest liberality allowed by a private English school would not have been a very close fit for a ten-year-old Seminole Indian. Incredible to picture him, "a fine, intelligent-looking boy, of a light copper colour" either attending classes in history, geography, French and German, mathematics, writing, and biblical lectures, the strange syllables coming awkwardly in English with a Seminole accent, or winter snow falling on the straight black hair during the odd moments of play at cricket or marbles.[60]

For three years Nikkanochee stayed at Mill Hill, forgetting the old ways as he became an adolescent. And then, presumably in compliance with Nikkanochee's wishes, the Reverend Mr. Sherman "apprenticed him to Messrs. R. & H. Green, the great shipowners who traded in those days with Australia. Osceola profited by his education, both ashore and afloat, and in due course became an officer in Messrs. Green's service, rising ... to the rank of first mate."[61]

How must it have been for him? High in the rigging of a sailing ship bound for Australia, half a world away from home? And then one day, with his ship in port, he was ordered to his cabin by the captain to write a letter home. Undetected, he slipped through the porthole and swam to shore. "Rumor had it that he turned up at the gold diggings in Australia but this was never confirmed. ... Presumably the young Red Indian settled in that land of opportunity on the far side of the world. Or did he perhaps return to the land of his ancestors? Who knows? But possibly, somewhere in the world today, there is living another small boy whose family legend has it that he is descended from the last of the Seminoles."[62]

And what of Andrew Welch? Through this last decade of his life he developed and continued what the British medical directory called a "most successful" practice. He once claimed that "for the sake of his health [he] felt it requisite to return to America." No record of his having done so can be found, and again, the tax records consistently indicate that he was basically in residence in London until his death there in 1852.[63] But during this time he did not rest content with medicine alone, though he took in as a partner John Dalston

Jones in 1847, and shortly before his death his own son, Henry.⁶⁴ The injured, the young, the downtrodden were still to be healed and helped, their plights recorded.

A few years after his return to England, while on a visit to the city of Worcester, he met on the street a black man handing out religious tracts. Worcester, a small county town on the Severn River, 100 miles west of London, provided scanty enough subsistence for its able-bodied citizens and something less for a lone Negro, a stranger, in poor health and with no skill or trade. Rather than salve his conscience with a coin, Welch invited the forlorn figure to visit him.

The man's name was Benjamin Benson. According to his account, he had been born into slavery in Bermuda on December 16, 1818. He carried a knife scar over his left eye and a brand on his right shoulder, identifying marks given him by his owners before the age of ten. His story, as related to Dr. Welch, was no more and no less dreadful than those of other victims of this peculiarly human institution. He had been sold away from his mother at the age of twelve and was passed from owner to owner through the years, living in Mobile, New Orleans, North Carolina, and then back in Bermuda where, with all other slaves within the British colonies, he was set free on August 1, 1834.⁶⁵ Again he went to sea, returning eventually to America where he was re-enslaved.

Escaping a year later, he stowed away on a ship bound for Nassau. He shipped from port to port, finally leaving ship, with references from the captain, in England. Later he worked as a miner, waiter, and finally, as Welch had found him, he was selling religious tracts on the streets of Worcester.

In an article dealing with Welch's work on ringworm (and evidently without reference to Welch's other writings), the author, William Brockbank, refers to Welch as "flamboyant" and "something of a showman."[66] This view can only be confirmed in Welch's trip to Charleston with Jane Johns, the bringing of an Indian boy to London, and now his association with Benjamin Benson, who "accompanied the writer [Welch] in his visits to several other towns."[67] But acknowledging his "showmanship" is not to demean his effort. The nineteenth century was an age of showmen, and words like "biggest," "smallest," "best," and "worst" became criteria by which to measure not only physical phenomena but the habits of man. Social changes once debated by gentlemen were now being shouted in the streets by mobs. Every man who might have made a social or political comment seemed to feel that sincerity could be indicated only by stretching his thoughts to fill a pamphlet. If he had evidence to exhibit, so much the better. The tavern sign that once led a traveler to rest would grow to a million square feet, the voices raised against inhumanity would become, a century later, a televised chorus advertising deodorant. Advertising had been born.

And perhaps the excesses of today can better be borne when one considers that the "advertising" of Andrew Welch and his contemporaries undeniably played a part in bringing the grosser injustices of the times to the attention of statesman and soldier alike; for government and army, having brought about the problems, would likewise be called upon to cure them. The United States would continue the destruction of the American Indian for another half-century, but against a growing tide of opposition. And though the narratives of Jane Johns, Nikkanochee, and Benjamin Benson did not strike the sparks of an *Uncle Tom's Cabin*, still they may have played their parts in bringing about the social climate that would allow such political expedients as the Emancipation Proclamation to stand.

Certainly Welch spoke no word of good for the Indians in *The Narrative of Jane Johns*. As to Negroes and slavery, he said nothing at all, unless it can be assumed that his references to "a carriage and driver belonging to Colonel James Dell" referred to a Negro slave whose name and condition were not worth mentioning, though he took the same risk as the others in going after Mrs. Johns. He did condone the reference by the Reverend Mr. Brown to the Negroes who butchered the wounded after Dade's battle as "a troop of

INTRODUCTION. *xliii*

deeply darker fiends [who triumphed] over a fallen foe, which living they had not dared to face!"⁶⁸ But four years later his thinking would have been altered to the extent that he would publish *Nikkanochee*, a veritable philippic against Indian extermination. Six more years, and he would strike out in opposition to the slavery he had once ignored.

James Andrew Welch died on January 20, 1852, at the age of fifty-four. His body lies beneath a marble block in the churchyard of St. John-at-Hackney, just a half-mile from where he lived.

Welch once wrote of goals. "I ... confess ... the hope ... that my humble name may ... be registered with those ... who have ... abridged the sufferings of afflicted humanity."

FRANK LAUMER.

Talisman.
Dade City, Florida.

NOTES.

1. *The British Medical Directory for England, Scotland, and Wales* (London, 1853), p. 561. The story of the ordeal of Jane Johns was published simultaneously in Charleston (printed by Burke and Giles, 1837) and in Baltimore (Lucas and Deaver, 1837), though a difference in paging in the two volumes suggests another edition. As far as is known, only the single original editions of *A Narrative of the Early Days and Remembrances of Oceola Nikkanochee* and of *A Narrative of the Life of Benjamin Benson* were printed.

INTRODUCTION.

2. For virtually all information concerning Andrew Welch in England the author is indebted to the incredible research of his brother Marsh, whose information in almost daily letters from England totaled more than 20,000 words. Specific sources for that information will be given hereafter as conveyed in personal letters from Marsh Laumer to Frank Laumer from January 14, 1976 through March 20, 1976. The birth record of Andrew Welch was found in the parish registers at the vicarage of Nazeing Church.

3. Genealogical information on the Welch family was supplied by Mrs. Andrew Davies Welch, Callis-2 Bumble's Green, Nazeing, Essex.

4. Through the years Welch changed residence several times (Kingsland Place, Dalston, and Shoreditch, all in the borough of Hackney), and the confusion is heightened by the fact that his address might be listed by street in one record while under the name of a building or section of town in another record. However all addresses are within a few blocks of each other.

5. Record book of "Marriages solemnized in the parish of St. Leonard, Shoreditch, in the county of Middlesex in the year 1819," is in the search room of the County Hall, repository of the greater London council records.

6. Register of Baptisms of St. Leonard, Shoreditch, County Hall. Jane Welch died the first week in April 1831, at the age of eleven years. St. Leonard burial records.

7. Register of Baptisms of St. Leonard, Shoreditch.

8. Ibid. Register of burials for St. Leonard, Shoreditch.

9. Obituary, *The British Medical Directory for England, Scotland and Wales* (London, 1853), p. 561.

10. Andrew Welch, *A Narrative of the Early Days and Remembrances of Oceola Nikkanochee* (London, 1841), p. 194.

11. Welch, *A Narrative of the Life of Benjamin Benson* (London, 1847), p. iv. Emphasis added.

12. Deed Book C, entries 445, 471, Duval County records, Jacksonville, Florida, of Harold Davies of Title and Trust Company of Florida, 200 E. Forsyth St., Jacksonville. The courthouse copies of these records were destroyed in the Jacksonville fire of May 1901.

13. Frances Mary Ann died February 17, 1876, at the

INTRODUCTION.   xlv

age of seventy-seven. The dates are inscribed on the Welch tomb at the church of St. John-at-Hackney.

14. St. Johns County Court Records, St. Augustine, Vol. I, County L-5, item 91.

15. James M. Gould, "Dr. Andrew Welsh," St. Augustine *Florida Herald and Southern Democrat*, July 24, 1853. This long and interesting editorial as well as other contemporary newspaper pieces which opened new avenues in the search for Andrew Welch, were discovered and brought to the attention of the author by Dr. E. Ashby Hammond of the University of Florida.

16. Gesborne Henry Welch, born 1814, died 1880, in America. Gesborne (also spelled Gisben and Gisborne) was the son of Andrew's older brother, John Davies Welch, according to the Welch family tree. On July 4, 1838, Gesborne was involved in a land transfer of Welch's Florida property, Deed Book "C", entries 444 and 445, Duval County Records, Jacksonville, Florida.

17. Governor William P. DuVal to Thomas L. McKenney, February 22, 1826, Clarence E. Carter, ed., *The Territorial Papers of the United States*, vol. 23, *The Territory of Florida, 1824–1828* (Washington, D.C., 1958), pp. 445–46.

18. St. Augustine *Florida Herald and Southern Democrat*, July 24, 1843.

19. Ibid.

20. Ibid.

21. *Jacksonville Courier*, n.d., quoted in Welch, *Jane Johns*, p. 27.

22. Welch, *Jane Johns*, p. 9.

23. W. A. Thorburn, curator, Scottish United Services Museum, The Castle, Edinburgh, to Frank Laumer, September 12, 1963.

24. St. Augustine *Florida Herald and Southern Democrat*, July 24, 1843.

25. Savannah *Daily Georgian*, February 16, 1837.

26. Ibid.

27. Ibid., February 20, 1837.

28. *Charleston Courier*, March 2, 1837.

29. Major Francis S. Belton to General Duncan L. Clinch, January 5, 1836, Record group 391, selected pages of Orderly Book, 1834–38, Company B, 2nd Artillery; Lieu-

tenant John C. Casey to Thomas Basinger, J. 1836, quoted by Edward P. Lawton, *A Saga of the South* (Fort Myers Beach, Fla., Island Press, 1965), p. 139.

30. *United States Military Reservations, National Cemeteries, and Military Parks* (Washington: Government Printing Office, 1916), p. 376.

31. Welch, *Jane Johns*, p. 11.

32. Savannah *Daily Georgian*, April 15, 1837.

33. Welch, *Nikkanochee*, p. 124.

34. Deed Book "C", entry 425, Duval County Records, Jacksonville.

35. St. Augustine *Florida Herald*, August 4, 1838.

36. Welch, *Nikkanochee*, pp. 124–25.

37. Letter to Welch from Citizens of Jacksonville, January 23, 1837, given in *Jane Johns*, pp. 28–29.

38. Welch, *Nikkanochee*, p. 126.

39. Ibid., p. 131.

40. Ibid., p. 181.

41. Ibid., p. 190.

42. Ibid., pp. 182–86.

43. St. Augustine *Florida Herald*, August 4, 1838.

44. Welch, *Nikkanochee*, pp. 190–91.

45. Ibid., p. 192.

46. Ibid.

47. Ibid.

48. Ibid., p. 194.

49. It was with a certain shock that the author discovered, after completing the first draft of this introduction, that there were, indeed, *three* Dr. Welches. The Welch family tree lists two older brothers of James Andrew as doctors. This alone complicates the record, but an added surprise was one doctor brother was also named Andrew. Though internal evidence in all the writings considered here seem to relate to one man, James Andrew Welch, there is need for further investigation.

50. *Tinea Capitis*, p. x.

51. Gesborne Welch is assumed to have remained in America. As late as 1894 the lands associated with Andrew Welch were still being sold, the instrument of sale signed by Andrew J. Welch, perhaps a son of Gesborne. No trace of the family beyond that date has been found.

INTRODUCTION.

52. Welch, *Nikkanochee*, p. 195.
53. Ibid., p. 217. The orginal of this painting hangs in the Nelson Gallery of Art, Kansas City, Missouri. A photoreproduction is included in the facsimile edition here along with the original frontispiece.
54. Letter to E. Hampden-Cook from grandson of Reverend James Sherman (name illegible), September 26, 1912, Mill Hill College files.
55. D. G. Goyder, ed., *Phrenological Almanac* (Glasgow, Issue No. 1, 1842).
56. H. C. Donovan to E. Hampden-Cook, March 10, 1913, Mill Hill College files.
57. Reverend James Sherman, *A Memoir of Mrs. Sherman* (London, Charles Gilpin, 1848), p. 257.
58. Welch, *Nikkanochee*, preface.
59. "Profile—Prince Oceola Nikkanochee Econchatti," *Mill Hill Magazine*, no. 488, vol. 103, no. 2. (spring 1975), p. 42.
60. Ibid.
61. Letter from grandson of the Reverend Mr. Sherman to Hampden-Cook, Mill Hill College files.
62. "Profile", *Mill Hill Magazine.*
63. From the Welch tomb in the churchyard of St. John-at-Hackney; "James Andrew Welch, Dalston, 20 Jan 1852, aged 53."
64. Henry James Wadsworth Welch was admitted to the Royal College of Surgeons in 1847. *The British Medical Directory*, 1853.
65. Helen Rex Keller, *The Dictionary of Dates* (New York, Macmillan Co., 1934), p. 457.
66. William Brockbank, "A Popular Treatise on Tinea Capitas, by J. A. Welch, 1837," *Medical History*, 6:386–88.
67. Welch, *Benjamin Benson*, p. 35.
68. Sermon by the Reverend David Brown in St. Augustine, November 1836, quoted in Welch, *Jane Johns*, p. 22.

THE

EARLY DAYS AND REMEMBRANCES

OF

OCEOLA NIKKANOCHEE,

PRINCE OF ECONCHATTI.

NIKKANOCHEE, PRINCE OF ECONCHATTI,

A young Seminole Indian.

SON OF ECONCHATTI-MICO, KING OF THE RED HILLS.

A NARRATIVE

OF THE

EARLY DAYS AND REMEMBRANCES

OF

OCEOLA NIKKANOCHEE,

PRINCE OF ECONCHATTI,

A YOUNG SEMINOLE INDIAN; SON OF ECONCHATTI-MICO, KING OF THE RED HILLS, IN FLORIDA;

WITH

A BRIEF HISTORY OF HIS NATION, AND HIS RENOWNED UNCLE, OCEOLA, AND HIS PARENTS:

AND

AMUSING TALES, ILLUSTRATIVE OF INDIAN LIFE IN FLORIDA.

"This child, who parentless, is therefore mine."
BYRON.

WRITTEN BY HIS GUARDIAN.

LONDON:
HATCHARD AND SON, PICCADILLY,
AND SOLD BY ALL BOOKSELLERS IN LONDON.

1841.

London—Printed by A. Drew, 17, Portugal Street, Lincoln's Inn.

TO THE

HONOURABLE THE COMMITTEE

OF THE

𝔄boriginеs' 𝔓rotection 𝔖ociety.

GENTLEMEN,

THE benevolent designs of your Society in behalf of the untaught children of the wilderness, are in themselves sufficient to insure some attention to this Book, more particularly when I assert that it has been written exclusively for the benefit of one who claims a high rank among his people, and who is in every way deserving the kind attention he daily experiences from the most distinguished characters of this country.

DEDICATION.

As a production, I hesitate to submit it to the perusal of gentlemen as famous for their literary attainments as for their philanthropy; but as a work penned for the motive already specified, as well as of bringing this high-born Child of Nature into the notice of that grade of society to which he undoubtedly belongs by birth and parentage, I fearlessly venture to dedicate to you my very humble effort.

With a high sense of admiration for your noble exertions to relieve the sufferings, and at the same time to enlighten the minds, of the Aborigines of all nations, and with an earnest prayer to the great Giver of life and reason that he may be pleased to crown your undertakings with success,

I have the honour to be,

GENTLEMEN,

With much respect,

Your devoted Servant,

THE AUTHOR.

PREFACE.

In compiling the following Narrative, I had no intention of bringing it before the public,—my object was to record all the events relating to the life and capture of my *protegée* with which I was acquainted; as much as I could obtain from himself, and from the report of the soldiers by whom he was taken; in order, that in the event of my death, the manuscript might inform him of his origin and history, and at the same time remind him of one who loved him with the fondness of a father. In compliance, however, with the urgent requests of many who take a warm interest in behalf of this young nobleman—for such he may in truth be called—and whose opinions and wishes I am bound to treat with respect, I am induced to publish it.

PREFACE.

To write the Biography of one in years, as dictated by himself, whose memory is rife with all the incidents of his existence since the first dawnings of memory — and of one who probably possesses the advantages of education; or the life of some eminent character, whose history may be gleaned, in a great measure, from publications, which have ever elucidated the most trifling act or circumstance connected with his private or public career—thus leaving the Historian little more than the trouble of compiling what is already known to the greater proportion of an intelligent community, may not be tasks of difficulty; but, to undertake the narration of events of one, not more than nine or ten years old; the most romantic and interesting of which have happened previous to the tender age of six or seven, and one who has, until that early time of his life, passed his days in a vast wilderness—whose intellects have scarcely been allowed to expand beyond the pale of instinct peculiar to all creatures in savage life— is an undertaking fraught with embarrassment: yet, in this I am sustained by the purity and innocence

PREFACE.

of my young *protegées* whose regard for truth is as remarkable as his brilliancy of conception, and clearness of expression.

More than three years have elapsed since Almighty Providence first consigned this interesting Orphan to my protection, and amply do I think myself rewarded for any attention and kindness my humble means have enabled me to bestow upon him, in the solace of having wrested one so amiable and helpless from ignorance, famine, toil, and wretchedness—to become, I trust, in future years, an ornament to civilized society, and a useful member in the community of intellectual life.

It is not, however, without some diffidence that I submit my humble production to the ordeal of the press. Yet it would ill become me to shrink from my duty to the child of my adoption, and withhold what I hope and trust may be for his benefit, from a dread of displeasing the refined judgment of the critic, or of incurring the censures of the enemies of benevolence. I am not without the hope, also, that this little book may assist in exciting the attention of Englishmen to

PREFACE.

the sufferings of a most interesting part of the human family, hitherto strangely overlooked; and that the Boy himself may eventually become the instrument of diffusing Christianity and peace among the remnants of his race, *the only means* of saving the RED MAN from utter extinction.

THE AUTHOR.

GROSVENOR STREET,
April, 1841.

OF THE

SEMINOLE INDIANS.

"Man, only, mars kind nature's plan,
And turns the fierce pursuit on man."
SIR WALTER SCOTT.

THE Seminoles appear to be a mixed tribe, having sprung chiefly from the wandering Creeks and Muscogulgees, who formerly fled the persecutions of the western districts; they also formed alliances in Florida with the Appalachees, Yemassees, and others. In process of time this newly formed tribe increased in numbers, and settled on the banks of the Chattahoochee and Coaeta rivers, not far from the approaching encroachments of what are called civiziled men, or whites; unhappily, among this class there are never wanting individuals, who, from interested motives, are always ready to foment wars and disputes between the neighbouring Indian tribes.

Without doubt too, they themselves possess the same laudable incitements to war which stimulate their more enlightened brethren—ambition, jealousy, revenge, love of conquest or gain. From some or other of these causes the Appalachees were induced to take up arms against this new, but now formidable tribe, the Seminoles; at this time the latter held possession of the settlements on the rivers Suwanney, Mikkasukey, and Talahassee, while colonies sprang up in other quarters, forming nations equally independent, and almost as formidable as their neighbours.

The Seminole Indians have retained all the daring spirit and fortitude peculiar to their wild progenitors.—In the battle-field their prowess has ever been acknowledged by their white enemies; and like all brave people, much may be said of their forbearance, previous to the commencement of hostilities; and of their gratitude, even in war, to those from whom they had formerly received kindness.

It is true that Indians have, in common with other nations, their peculiar failings; but I do not hesitate to aver, that they rarely commit a single act which comes within *their code of crimes*, but at the instigation of civilized men; either through base example, or by the introduction of that poison of the mind and body, ARDENT SPIRITS.

Formerly an Indian's word could be taken with confidence, even for his return within a given time, to undergo the sentence of death— the great Regulus could have done no more— and to this day such instances of romantic honour and fortitude in these uneducated sons of the forest, are by no means rare.

They are ferocious and relentless in battle, at times it must be confessed, sparing neither age nor sex; but they are early taught to estimate every act of carnage towards their foes as a virtue; and the very scalps produced at their council fires, are there viewed as commendable and honourable trophies; and are greeted by them with as much respect as captured flags and banners, when exhibited at the cities of Washington or London. It must be borne in mind, that the scalp is taken only after the *death* of the vanquished, as a proof of the success of the conqueror, and a warrior is estimated according to the number he possesses.

With regard to scalping, to which the Indians attach not the least ideas of cruelty, or even impropriety, with deep sorrow I avow it is not unfrequently practised by the whites, who can have no plea for such an act—and under circumstances too, which cannot fail of exciting our strongest disgust. Portions of skin have been cut from the bodies of Indians, and hung up in the houses of white men, as proofs of prowess—portions of the same have been converted into razor-strops; and I once shrunk with horror—not at the sight of a scalp, but that such a trophy should have been exhibited by the hand of a beautiful and highly-accomplished girl, in a drawing room, who triumphantly boasted that her brother had severed it from the head of an Indian enemy!!

It is hardly necessary to say that Indians are as susceptible of kindness as they are revengeful of injuries; my intimate acquaintance with them, has inspired me with a high respect for their social and domestic character. I will mention one or two instances in their favour, out of many:—At Dade's battle, one hundred and twelve, out of one hundred and fourteen of the white soldiers, under the command of Major Dade, were killed. One of the survivors was about being despatched by a Seminole, when, after the Indian had refused the soldier's proffered money, he recollected that he had recently assisted him in fitting a handle to his axe: even this simple act of civility was remembered by the red man, and proved the means of saving the life of an enemy.

Another instance of gratitude in Indian life, of a more prominent character, came under my personal observation. Previous to the war, many of the Seminole Tribe were in the habit of visiting me, at my plantation, on the banks of the river St. John. Among my red friends, were two sub-chiefs, who, with their wives and children, were invariably treated with that urbanity and kindness, due to their station and respectable deportment.

These worthy people generally came accompanied by others of the tribe, who never failed to bring with them some token of gratitude for the attention shewn them by my wife and myself; such as presents of venison, wild turkey, &c. It was not long subsequent to this good understanding that the war took place, and the consequent burning and destruction of property. The whole neighbourhood fled from the terrible vengeance of the maltreated Indians, and I, with others, deemed it better to abandon my property, fearing the incursion of some of the tribe, who might not have been aware of my friendly feeling towards them.

Not long after the departure of myself and family, two extensive establishments, one within a quarter of a mile, and the other not more than one mile from my residence, were burned to the ground by Indians. Yet, although they came to my house, and cooked food at my hearth, they injured nothing. Five years have elapsed since that period, and to this day my property has suffered but by the common ravages of time upon unoccupied buildings; and I feel assured I could have continued to live in safety in my "sweet retirement" to the present moment, but from the risk of strange Indians, whose wives or children had fallen sacrifices to the unsparing hands of the white dwellers upon the Indian frontier.

Englishmen have hitherto known little or nothing of these people; but in defiance of all prejudices against what are called savages— people differing so widely in their customs and political institutions from ourselves (which, be it remembered, are well and wisely adapted to their mode of life) my own experience leads me to the conclusion, that viewing vice and crime, as felt and acknowledged by each race—if I am not greatly mistaken, infinitely less will be found connected with that state of existence which we are apt to look upon as inferior.

With regard to America generally, I do not mean to imply that the feeling of prejudice against Indians, extends throughout the United States; on the contrary, I feel assured that young Oceola would have been as warmly received in New York or Boston, as he has been in London.

The accounts of all travellers who have visited Indians in their native wilds, as well as the histories by the first discoverers in America, unite in proving that the Almighty Creator of us all, has endowed his red children with moral and physical qualities of the highest order of excellence; their intelligence also is remarkable. It is melancholy to contemplate their wasting, to use their own language, "like snow before the sun." They seem only to require proper means, to recover that state of happiness they possessed when unmolested and uncontaminated by the white man.

Before the "Armed Boot" supplanted the Moccassin on the shores of America, their's appears to have been a "golden age"—unrestrained by laws of any denomination, their actions were guided solely by the dictates of virtue—crime was then unknown—and when the bonds of society were in the least violated, to have merited the contempt of a high-souled, chivalric people, was sufficient punishment for the offender; and such is the state of society, as it at present exists among those tribes who dwell near the base of the Rocky Mountains, who have not yet come under the pale of civilization.

Mr. Catlin, in his interesting lectures upon "the manners and customs of the North American Indians," describes the primitive tribes as ignorant of vice of any description; he dwelt many years among them, and declares, that during the whole period he was universally treated with hospitality and kindness—that they never stole from him to the value of a shilling; but that on his parting with them, they loaded him with presents, and consigned him to the care of the "Great Spirit."

My fancy is always fired, and my imagination kindles, as I dwell upon the wrongs and sorrows of these people.

Notwithstanding the vices which have been introduced among the Seminoles, there is something in the erect and manly form—in the proud bearing and confident demeanour, and in the graceful movements of the males, which impresses the eye of the beholder, and seems to remind him that they are the legitimate proprietors of the soil, from which their more enlightened neighbours are endeavouring to eject them.

A cursory glance at the policy pursued by the American Government, and by individuals towards the aborigines of this country, will convince the most indifferent observer that they have been unjustly used, and basely calumniated.

Some apology may be found for the present generations in Florida, in the circumstance, that they or their immediate ancestors have suffered much in their struggles and desperate encounters with them, while preparing for themselves a home in the wilderness; and it is natural that they should feel risings of indignation against a race of men, with whom they have been almost constantly at war; since, at such times, men are not accustomed to regard the justice or injustice of the origin of their quarrels, but throw the burden of blame upon their enemies.

But when a few more centuries shall have passed away—when the tales of cruelty practised upon present and former generations shall have become mitigated and softened by the lapse of time—when the present excited feelings shall have subsided, and when distance from the scene shall have mellowed down the light reflected from the funeral pyres, erected by the Red Man for their civilized encroachers—then will posterity view them in their true light,—and future ages, instead of wondering at their "inhuman barbarities," will be more surprised that *one* of them continued an ally of the whites, or that one magnanimous or generous deed was ever extended towards the intruders on their soil.

If the Indians were cruel—posterity will see that they were cruelly provoked by those claiming to be Christians;—If they were revengeful—that they only followed the example of the white man, who not only indulged in the same unhallowed passions, but who added avarice, rapine, and debauchery to their list of crimes.

If the Red Man retaliated injuries, the provocation had been tenfold on the part of the whites; who pursued them on their own soil, and through their native forests, with all the rapacity with which the half famished wolf pursues his prey.

I know of no objects that have a higher claim upon the sympathies of the world, than the remnants of these, once formidable tribes, scattered over the broad surface of America; now fast disappearing before the onward march of emigration and civilization. How striking the contrast! These men, lords of the soil they once held undisputed as their birthright, —where they roamed in all the majesty of uncultivated, yet, noble human nature—are now become objects of oppression and extermination.

We shudder when we call to mind, tales to which we listened in early boyhood, of Indian cruelties; but can our riper years find no palliation? Read the language of the Red Man, and then say if his cruelties were ever commensurate with the ingratitude of the whites.—" We took you by the hand" say they, "and bade you welcome to sit down by our side, and live with us as brothers—but how did you requite our kindness? You at first asked only a little of our land—we gave it—you requested more—it was given,—but not satisfied with this, you would monopolize the game of our forest—you seized upon all our most pleasant places, and drove us from the hunting and burial grounds of our sires!"

Their language is emphatically true; although by the laws of nations, the discoverers of this Continent claimed a right to take possession and plant colonies in the, then, wilds of America; they were cruelly unjust to seize upon the places which had been to the Indians the homes of their ancestors, and had descended to themselves. As they slowly and sullenly retired from " their pleasant places," the whites pressed hard upon them, and ever since the day they first granted them a "little land," they have been following their retreating footsteps, like the advancing billows of an angry ocean.

When we reproach the Indians with inhumanity in their mode of warfare—do we reflect that they are but uncivilized men,—that their ideas of right are rendered sacred by practice and tradition, handed down from time immemorial? If civilized nations rise *as one man,* when their rights are invaded or their territories encroached upon; is it matter of surprise that untaught Indians turn their tomahawks against the whites, when they endeavour to deprive them of that which they regarded as most sacred and dear?

As for cruelty, you will in vain search for examples among the traditions and annals of the past, to exceed those imposed upon the Red Man by the Whites, or to which their Indian allies have been instigated and encouraged; through which means, they sought to rid themselves of the odium of barbarity.

In reading of the rise and fall of civilized nations, with all the attendant wrongs and oppressions, our indignation becomes excited. Yet a relation of the wrongs and usurpations of civilized men over the confiding Indians of America, is a relation far more replete with cruelty—they have not only been deprived of their rights, but have been degraded in soul and body, and now, alas! are fading away, forgotten, to their graves, or, if perchance remembered—only to be stigmatized as "brutal savages."

It may be necessary, before we give an account of the family of the young Prince, to observe, that no name is ever bestowed by Indians, upon a young Iste-Chatti, or Red Child, without some particular meaning attached to it; which name, is often changed in after years, to one corresponding better to the age or circumstances of maturity; thus an infant may be called Green-bush, from its having first drawn breath beneath that verdant screen of nature. Another will be named Oceola, Rising Sun —Hutte-chumba, Evening-Star— Nathle-oce, Setting Moon—according to the time of its birth. And when arrived at " Man's Estate," in consequence of some peculiarity or physical structure, he will be spoken of as, Ulwe, tall—Chatqua, small—Saputhatkee, light; or by some act of heroism, either with a human enemy or one no less ferocious, he may be invested with a more formidable appellation, as, Catsha, tiger—Yaha, wolf—Halputta, alligator, &c.

The meaning of Nikkanochee, the name conferred upon the subject of this narrative by his Indian relations, I have hitherto been unable to discover. Oceola and Econchatti, I have added to his given name, that he may bear in remembrance, he is nephew and son of two of the most noble and distinguished Chiefs, the Floridas perhaps ever yet produced.

THE CHIEF OCEOLA.

"The steady brain, the sinewy limb,
To leap, to climb, to dive, to swim;
The iron frame, inured to bear
Each dire inclemency of air."
SIR WALTER SCOTT.

"Brief, brave, and glorious was his young career."
BYRON.

From the preceding account of the Seminole Indians, my reader will be in some measure prepared for the introduction of a character of the greatest renown in Florida; of whom, both as a man and as a warrior, but one opinion is entertained by his friends and his enemies. Conspicuous among his own nation for his courage and his bodily strength, he rendered himself no less the terror of the pale-faces during war, than he was universally known to

OCEOLA the CELEBRATED CHIEF of the SEMINOLES,
UNCLE TO PRINCE ECONCHATTI.

Published by Hatchard & Son, Piccadilly.

have been generous and kind, previous to the commencement of hostilities—he was a husband and a father, but all that is known of his family, subsequent to his death, is, that they, with other Indian prisoners, underwent the sentence of banishment to the " Far West."

It is gratifying to know, that at present at least, a scion from so noble a stock has been saved from the ruthless destroyers of himself and his tribe; the boy whom I have been the happy means of preserving, being the son of Oceola's sister.

It has frequently been asserted in the United States of America, that Oceola, the great Master Spirit of the Seminoles, was of mixed blood. Some have declared him to be half Spanish—others that his father was an Englishman, named Powel—another has given the honor of his being, to a Scotchman, whilst some have asserted that he received an education at the Military College at West Point, in the State of New York, and consequently that he was thoroughly conversant with the English language. The tribe from which this renowned Chief sprang, has been as freely discussed; some have attributed his birth to the Creek nation—others to the Mikkasookies, and a few to the Cherokees.

From the warm interest I have at all times taken in matters concerning Indians, I have been induced to investigate cautiously, their manners, customs and history. The former, are open to any observing character, who will be at the pains of visiting them in their abodes, when not engaged in war. When at peace, they are kind and hospitable, and are willing to impart any information to the curious traveller. Their history is but little known, owing to the few intelligent whites, who are sufficiently acquainted with their language. Yet, almost every one, who has in any manner, associated with Indians, pretends to a knowledge of their general character, and is proud to be considered a good authority.

Judging from all I have been enabled to learn of the Chief Oceola from other Indians, and from respectable white men, who knew him from childhood, he was undoubtedly, a thorough-bred Seminole. I am borne out in this opinion by Mr. Catlin, who is probably, better acquainted with the physical, as well as moral structure of these people, than any other white man living; he painted an excellent likeness of this celebrated warrior, only four days previous to his death, in a prison at Charleston, South Carolina: which picture, stands conspicuous amidst hundreds of other portraits of Indians, in the elaborate collection, now exhibiting at the Egyptian Hall. Mr. Catlin, of course, had as fair an opportunity of forming a judgment, by the countenance of Oceola, as most men; he informs me, that his general appearance, and character, was that of a thorough-bred wild Indian, and that he did not seem, even to comprehend the English language.

But little became known to the white inhabitants of America, of the valorous spirit of Oceola, until the commencement of the unhappy Seminolee war, previous to which, when only a youth, he had distinguished himself among his own people, in some severe battles with the neighbouring tribes.

In the intermediate space of time, he seems to have led the wandering, careless life of a hunter, when his only opportunities of signalizing himself, were in his perilous encounters with the prowling monsters of the forest, to which he often proved a mortal enemy.

It was not until the latter end of the year 1835, that the energies of Oceola were roused into full vigor. At this time an effort was made by the Pseudo-Americans—the whites,—to expatriate the true lords of the soil, from the homes of their fathers, and send them away to the " far west;" where thousands had already perished by change of climate, grief, or dissentions with the different tribes, who had been mercilessly huddled together by treacherous mock treaties, on lands insufficient in extent and quality, to supply game and other necessaries, on which, they had hitherto depended in the more congenial climes of the South; consequently wars ensued among themselves, which, with the aid of whiskey, plentifully supplied by their Christian neighbours, soon reduced their numbers.

In December, 1835, a meeting or "Talk," as it is expressed by Indians, was held at Camp King, at which two hundred and fifty red warriors assembled, met by a battalion of white soldiers, under command of General Clinch, who was accompanied by several other officers of distinction.

A council of Indians, held in their native wilds, upon the green carpet of nature, under the broad canopy of heaven, is, to a reflecting mind, a spectacle replete with solemnity and interest. The wide expanding, densely-foliaged oak, from whose thousand branches, hang in the beauty of neglected nature, in festoons and strips of many feet, the moss, peculiar to the southern States of North America—the stately pine—the sturdy hickory—and the splendid magnolia—all lend their aid to blend in the *coup d'œil*, a fitting place for purpose deep.

In scenes similar to this, the chiefs and elders meet to determine the course to be adopted in all cases of emergency; here the small remnant of a powerful and warlike tribe, met to decide upon peace or war, in which millions of civilized men, with all the arts and implements of battle, were pitted against a few hundreds of poor persecuted Indians.

On one side of the conclave alluded to, sat in purse-proud state, General Wiley Thompson, one of those subtle minions of power, who are appointed by Congress, as agents from the United States, to treat with Indians for purchase or exchange of lands; at the same time he is expected to protect the tribe, he thus becomes attached to, from wrongs and oppressions of the neigbbouring whites, and report to the government a true and impartial statement of the negociation he is empowered to conduct.

This appointment would be considered, by one unacquainted with the general character of Indian agents, a post of some respectability, and so it may be, when occupied by honest men; but in this instance, General Thompson opened a shop, for the purpose of trading with the aborigines, from which he issued Whiskey, Tomahawks, Spears, Gunpowder, and Rifles; thus providing in the first place, an incentive to their no less deadly weapons; in exchange for Otter-skins, Deer-skins, and Cattle-hides; articles easily conveyed to a northern market, by which he accumulated considerable wealth.

Independently of this villainous mode of traffic, wherein the Seminoles were invariably cheated, he employed many in laborious occupations, a neglect of which, insured them severe chastisement, summarily executed, by twisted strips of hide, applied to the bare skin, whilst the poor victim of oppression was bound to a tree. But the day of vengeance was at hand:—the very Rifle which Thompson had gratuitously presented to Oceola, with a view to conciliate him for cruelties inflicted upon his fellows, was the weapon, by which he expiated his manifold sins against this generous people.

After a preliminary address from General Clinch, seconded by General Thompson, setting forth the advantages of the treaty they wished to enforce, and to which some of the Indian Chiefs replied in their beautiful figurative language; a deed of contract, binding the Seminoles to give up their lands in Florida, to the United States' government, in exchange for others in a distant country, was placed upon the table, and application made to the principal warriors, to attach their thereunto. An imbecile old Chief, called Enematkla, was the first to declare himself a traitor to his tribe, by affixing his sign-manual; he was followed by a few others of inferior grade, until it was submitted to Oçeola, who, with all the pride of offended dignity thus offered to himself and his countrymen, with indignation sparkling in his eye, and a contemptuous curl of the lip, drew from his bosom a dagger, and with a countenance that seemed to strike terror into all by whom he was opposed, he hurled the trusty steel with such force into the hateful document, that it passed fairly through the table—exclaiming at the same time, "THERE IS MY MARK!!"

" All was so quick that it might seem,
" A flash of lightning, or a dream."

General Clinch thought this a *clincher;* Wiley Thompson looked more *wily,* and all the surrounding white men grew *whiter;* each stood aghast in astonishment, as the undaunted young hero firmly gripped the handle of his deeply buried weapon, and bade defiance to all the fully armed warriors, by whom he was encircled.

For this novel mode of signing with a *steel pen,* by which matters were so speedily brought to a *point,* Oceola was immediately seized upon, and so tightly bound to a tree, that the cords by which he was confined, cut deeply into the flesh;

OCEOLA'S MODE OF SIGNING THE TREATY

evidences of which were clearly exhibited when Mr. Catlin painted his likeness, two years subsequent to this disgraceful transaction. After being half suspended in this torturing position forty-eight hours, he was released to undergo the full penalty of his temerity : iron fetters now usurped the place of ropes, and solitary confinement was added to his overflowing cup of misery ! but nought at this time, could subdue the indomitable spirit of this high-souled Chief; he spurned their shackles, as he had defied their hempen bonds, and in all probability would have perished, rather than have yielded to such inhuman oppression; but he reflected that the fate of his tribe depended, in a great measure, upon his presence among them. This feeling of affection for his country, and his kindred, alone induced him to feign contrition for the alleged offence he had offered to the heads of a people calling themselves Christians.

In full confidence, that the cruelties inflicted upon Oceola, would operate as a warning to others of his tribe, he was liberated. It was not likely, that a soul sufficiently daring to have acted as he had done, could readily forgive the indignities so recently heaped upon him: no sooner was the captive free, than, with his companions in arms, who waited anxiously to receive him, he caused the deep forest to re-echo the well known WAR-WHOOP, as a signal for hostilities.

Enamatkla was forthwith shot as a traitor, and General Wiley Thompson, with five others who had the misfortune to be with him at the time, fell before their unerring rifles. Oceola first despatching Thompson, with the rifle I before stated he had offered as a present, to conciliate his determined enemy.

Oceola now sent a negro to General Clinch, to inform him that he possessed 150 barrels of gunpowder, which should all be consumed before his people could be conquered, and that he would lead the cheating 'pale-faces' a dance of five years, for their insolence towards himself and his warriors.

Although the brave Oceola did not live to see his prediction fulfilled, of leading the "pale-faces a dance of five years," yet true enough, this little band of warriors have maintained their ground for the time specified; at the loss of upwards of eighteen hundred men, and an expense of more than six millions sterling to the United States. In the battle of Ouithlacoochee, Oceola was known to have fought with desperate valour. At the same time that the woods resounded with peals of musketry, and the fierce, sharp cracks of the Indian rifles, accompanied by appalling war-whoops; his voice was distinctly heard, calling to his warriors

"Take away the wounded, never mind the dead!"

At Dade's battle, as it is denominated by the Americans, one hundred and twelve of the whites were killed by Indians, only two escaping out of one hundred and fourteen. These soldiers, commanded by Major Dade, were marching, fully armed, attended by a six-pounder cannon drawn by oxen, and a waggon containing arms and ammunition, through the heart of an enemy's country. Yet the killing of these men by the Seminoles, is stigmatized as a *Horrible Massacre*, and the memory of Dade revered as a martyr.—At the same time, *unarmed* Red Men, with their wives and children, were daily slaughtered—these were *Glorious Achievements!*

When the remains of Major Dade and his soldiers were discovered by the Americans, many days after this unfortunate circumstance, it was remarked, that not a single article of value was taken from the bodies—watches and valuable rings were found upon the officers, unmolested. The savage spurns to rob the dead! How many of these ornaments would have remained upon the bodies of *Indians*, under similar circumstances?

During a series of battles, in which the whites were invariably repulsed, Oceola signalized himself for good generalship and courage, and if, at any time he had recourse to stratagem, he was fully authorized in so doing, by the frequent treacherous attempts, made by his enemies, to entrap him.

On the 6th of October, 1836, the garrison at Fort Drane was so reduced for provisions, having been besieged for a length of time by the Indians, that the white troops were glad to hold a parley with Oceola, and invited him, through Captain Hitchcock, with a flag of truce, to approach the fort. In full confidence he came, attended by three hundred warriors; when he informed the Captain that he knew the soldiers were in a desperate state, bordering upon starvation, and that, at that moment, they were subsisting upon the flesh of horses and dogs; at the same time, he generously offered his enemies an ox and some brandy.

During this conference, General Clinch appeared with a strong reinforcement, and made an essay to capture the generous Oceola and his warriors, *in defiance of the flag of truce*, which he must have seen, as he was near enough to fire upon the Indians.

The liberty of this heroic young warrior was not of long endurance—one year more, and his brilliant career closed for ever! October 20th, 1837, was a day appointed for Oceola to meet General Hernandez, with a view to form some arrangement, by which this unjust war might be brought to a close. Accordingly, Oceola again appeared under a flag of truce, when, as is briefly described in a Florida newspaper— *"General Jessup so arranged the soldiers under command of General Hernandez; that, at a preconcerted signal, the whole of Oceola's band should be surrounded; which ruse de guerre was performed to admiration; when the crest-fallen hero of the Seminoles and his partizans laid down their rifles."* This statement is false—the Indians had not *laid down* their rifles, but had, according to agreement with General Hernandez, *placed them against a tree,* and as soon as the white troops showed themselves, they were immediately seized upon, leaving the Indians defenceless.

Thus fell into the hands of their treacherous enemies, the renowned, the brave, the good Oceola, with upwards of eighty of his principal warriors, together with *his wife and son (a young boy) and two other Indian women.*

> "The eagle-plumes droop o'er his piercing eyes,
> The fire of youth was there;—
> The fire of youth still brightened the look,
> But their lustre was dimm'd by despair."
>
> M. A. W.

Never was a more disgraceful piece of villainy perpetrated in a civilized land—the Americans have no plea, by which they can justify such a violation of the law of nations. As they had, throughout the war, and on all previous occasions, acknowledged the Seminoles as an independent people, by forming treaties with them, and receiving their chiefs as ambassadors, the government of the United States could not have considered them as rebels.

Poor Oceola! with his wife and child, and his brave followers, was confined but a short time in the fort at St. Augustine, in East Florida;

when, for the better security of the victims, the government ordered their removal to Sullivan's Island, near Charleston, and there—in a dungeon—the spirit of Oceola fled for ever!

There was a touching commentary on woman's worth, displayed in the dying hour of the Seminole Chieftain. The stern warrior, who had passed through life without having, in appearance, done aught to win the imperishable love of devoted woman, yet expired with his head pillowed on a female bosom.

Cold as the heart of the savage is supposed to be, in regard to the social and domestic feelings, the death-couch of Oceola yields triumphant evidence of the Indian's submission to the sway of the affections.

A captive, and to add to the bitterness of imprisonment, treacherously captured—smarting under a sense of his nation's many wrongs—feeling, that with his death was lost the sole chance for the deliverance of his people, from the avaricious power of the white man. It may well be conceived, that the soul of the Chief was filled with emotion, and that he had but few feelings to spare, in exercises of the love and sympathies of life.

But the power of woman mastered the keen remembrances of the Indian's manifold grievances, and the voice of his faithful wife, as she wiped from his brow the death damps, fell gratefully and soothingly upon the ebbing senses of the captive.

In witnessing the entire devotion, and patient love of his too wretched wife, the Indian forgot his injuries, and the indomitable spirit, so often flashing in the van of battle, passed away, with a murmur of love to her, the companion of his freedom, and the sharer of his prison!

DIRGE BY SEMINOLE WARRIORS.

Signed—LESLIE.

   Go to thy rest,—
Not where the green and tall magnolias bow,
Slowly and solemnly their lofty crests—
   Above the violet grass we lay thee now!

   Not where the pine
With dreary sighing answered back thy tread,
When forest dwellers made beneath its shrine,
   The ancient places of their silent dead,—

   Not where the stream
Beneath the arching wild vine, whispers low,
With spirit-voices—when the sun's last beam
   Falls, where it bathes the warrior's dust—we go.

   To thy dark bed
We would not, that *their* music's wail should come,
Nor see *them* bend the plumed and glittering head,
   In stately mourning to the deep-toned drum.

   They mock us well,—
With banner waving, and that hollow sound,
Long pealing from the battlements, to tell
   That *thou*, our brave, hast ransom found.

  Why should *they* grieve,
E'en while their pale blood curdles to the heart,
Beside thy grave,—that thou *their* bonds canst leave,
 And to our fathers' hunting fields depart?*

  We do not weep—
The Red Man hath no tear to shed for thee,—
Smiling, we gaze upon the dreamless sleep,
 The fortress broken, and the captive free.

  Hither we bring,
Ere yet this earth on thy cold brow we lay,
Thy Boy,—for one wild moment here to cling,
 In love's first sorrow, to those lips of clay.

  Bend low and near,—
Nor sigh, or moan must break our Chief's repose—
Yet, Boy—on thy young heart be written here,
 A deep and burning memory of his foes!

  We ask not fame,—
We call not vengeance for the faith we gave;
Trace in the language of your land his name,
 And show *your* sons the SEMINOLE'S GRAVE.

---

 * Indians believe that if they are brave and good in this world, they will be rewarded in the next by being placed in excellent hunting grounds.

The sympathy of the Americans for the death of Oceola ran so high, that they buried him with military honours due to a general; and, with a tardy appreciation of his character, indicative more of a puling sentimentality, than a love of justice, or admiration of his worth, they exalt their victim into a hero of romance.

Oceola was interred at Fort Moultrie, near Charleston;—over his grave is a handsome marble monument, on which is inscribed

OCEOLA.

I cannot take leave of this melancholy part of the narrative, without laying before my readers another beautiful piece of poetry, written by Alfred Street, an American; which, like the last, is full of fire, and breathes a manly and generous feeling towards the departed hero.

PART I.

The rich blue sky is o'er,
   Around are the tall green trees,
And the jessamine's breath from the everglade
   Is borne on the wandering breeze.
On the mingled grass and flowers
   Is a fierce and threat'ning form,
That looks like an eagle when pluming his wing
   To brave the gathering storm.

His rifle within his grasp—
   The bright plume o'er his head—
His features are clothed with a warrior's pride,
   And he moves with a monarch's tread.
He bends his listening ear,
   He peers through the tangled screen,
And he smiles with joy, as the flash of steel
   Through the everglade's grass is seen.

One wave of his stalwart arm,
    Wild forms around him stand,
And his eye glares bright with triumphant light,
    As he looks at his swarthy band.
Nearer the bayonets' gleam—
    At the edge of the *hammock now,
The pale-face ranks are rallying,
    But they seek in vain the foe.

They see in that lovely scene
    But the humming-bird o'er the flowers,
And the glittering wing of the paroquet
    In the cool and fragrant bowers.
But hark! from the cypress shade,—
    From the bay-tree's glossy leaves,
And the nooks where the vine from bough to bough,
    Its serpentine festoon weaves ;—

The loud, shrill warwhoops burst
    On the soft and sleeping air,
And quick, bright darts of surrounding death
    Are fearfully glancing there.
The eagle with fierce delight
    Abroad has his pinions cast,
And he shrinks as he bathes in the crimson rain,
    And sweeps through the whizzing blast.

---

* A hammock, or hummock, is a dense wood with thick jungle or under-brush.

The battle-storm is o'er—
    The hammock is reeking red—
But who looks there with victorious smile,
    On the heaps of the pale-face dead?
'Tis a tribe's young warrior Chief!
    The deeds of whose vengeful flame,
Have filled the ear of a mighty land
    With the terror of his name.

PART II.

In a dark and dungeon room
    Is stretched a mighty form,
And it shakes in its dreadful agony,
    Like a leaf in the autumn storm.
No pillar'd palmetto hangs
    Its tuft in the clear, bright air;
But a sorrowing group, and the narrow wall,
    And a smouldering hearth are there.

The white froth on his lip,
    His trembling, gasping breath,—
And the hollow rattle in his throat,
    Proclaim the conqueror—death.
'Tis the proud, victorious Chief,
    Who smiled 'mid the pale-face slain;
'Tis the eagle that swept through the whizzing blast,
    And bathed in the crimson rain.

For his own green forest home,
 He had struggled long and well;
But the soul that had breasted a nation's arms
 At the touch of a fetter, fell.
He had worn wild freedom's crown
 On his bright, unconquered brow,
Since he first saw the light of his beautiful skies:
 It was gone for ever now!

But still, in his last dread hour,
 Did not bright visions come!
Bright visions that shed a golden gleam
 On the darkness of his doom?
They calm'd his throbbing pulse,
 And they hung on his muttering breath;
The spray thrown up from life's frenzied flood
 Plunging on to the gulf of death.

The close walls shrunk away;—
 Above was the stainless sky,
And the lakes, with their floating isles of flowers,
 Spread glittering to his eye.
O'er his hut the live-oak spread
 Its branching, gigantic shade,
With its dots of leaves, and its robes of moss,
 Broad, blackening on the glade.

But a sterner sight is round,
    Battle's wild torrent is there,—
The tomahawk gleams, and the red blood streams,
    And the war-whoops rend the air.
At the head of his faithful band,
    He peals forth his terrible cry,
As he fiercely leaps 'mid the slaughtered heaps
    Of the foe, that but fought to die.

  * * * *

One gasp—and the eye is glazed,
    And still is the stiffening clay;
The eagle soul of the Chief had passed
    On the battle's flood away!

CAPTAIN GRAHAM AND NATHLEOCEE.

"What is country—name—fame—fortune—
When all powerful love steps in,
And wages war against them?"

I digress so far from the course of my narrative, as to introduce two personages, who may appear very much in the characters of a hero and heroine of romance; still, the circumstances of which I am about to speak, are facts, related to me by one intimately acquainted with Captain Graham, and by whom the following interesting tale was communicated.

John Graham, about three years previous to the Seminole war, arrived in St. Augustine, a

Lieutenant in a regiment of dragoons, where many a fair "southerner" sighed for the tall, athletic, yet graceful form of the fair-haired Officer, whose highly-polished manners corresponded well with his manly beauty; but the heart of young Graham was not to be taken by all the combined allurements of beauty, wealth, or high accomplishments. In vain they whirled the giddy mazes of the dance, or tried the more fascinating charms of music—he withstood the siege of a hundred gazelle eyes—yet remained firm and unsubdued, until ordered to the frontier encampment, on the Indian boundary line.

Here, in the wilds of nature, Graham felt a passion for the charms of perfect freedom in sylvan life. He remembered many tales in the romantic history of Scotland, the land of his forefathers, of clans headed by Chiefs of his own name, and compared their rude character with the Indians, with whom he was now destined to hold frequent intercourse; he was surprised to find a striking similarity in dress, and many of their manners and customs, to those of the ancient Highlanders.

He sought their society, and soon selected a young Chief, at this time of no great notoriety, as his friend, and almost constant companion. This bold and hardy warrior, then about the same age as himself, was no other than Oceola, whose subsequent deeds of valour and military discretion, astonished, and at the same time, struck admiration into the hearts of his enemies.

These young heroes soon established a friendship of no ordinary character—their hearts became as thoroughly amalgamated, as welded gold and silver—together they followed the chase, and many were "the hair-breadth 'scapes" and toils endured by these singularly contrasted specimens of civilized refinement, and rude, yet haughty grandeur of savage life.

Than Graham, a more perfect specimen of manly beauty—chivalric bearing—and gentlemanly deportment, could seldom be realized—few maidens could have resisted the soft blandishments of his addresses.

Oceola was tall, and of a spare habit—his limbs were well proportioned, and his complexion of the olive-red peculiar to his tribe—his features were not decidedly handsome, yet on scrutinizing his face, there was nothing with which one could be dissatisfied—his teeth were regular—his nose rather Grecian than otherwise—but the eye! "that herald of the soul"—was, in itself, constituted to command; when under excitement, it flashed fury and stern resolve—but when aiding its alluring ally, the well-formed mouth, in a smile—it warmed the very heart of its beholder with its beams of kindness.

It was on one of those glowing evenings of the sunny south, when the clouds are gilded in splendour, to await the departing god of light—after a hard day's toil, in pursuit of a tiger, which at last fell wounded by the rifle of Graham, and was finally despatched by the tomahawk of his swarthy friend, that the young officer first experienced the witchery of love.

Wearied and feverish from excitement, in a climate to which his system had searcely yet become reconciled, he gladly accepted the proffered hammock of netted grass, suspended by Nathleocee, Oceola's niece, beneath the umbrageous, wide-spreading branches of a large oak tree, from whose limbs hung the graceful, yet melancholy looking moss—at times in festoons, at others, falling in perpendicular masses, to the length of eight or ten feet; forming a drapery, infinitely surpassing, in beauty and splendour, all the richest and most elaborate works of art.

In this simple, yet ingeniously constructed aerial couch, the young hunter reposed his weary limbs, whilst Nathleocee watched his disturbed sleep, and amused her busy fancy with his delirious mutterings, in a language she could not comprehend; whilst she carefully, with a fan made from the feathers of the pinnawaw, or wild turkey, brushed away the intrusive mosquitoes, or the no less annoying sand flies.

After a few hours repose, Captain Graham awoke refreshed, and turning his still half-closed eyes, they rested upon a face of beauty, of so peculiar a character, and in such perfect accordance with his own romantic disposition, that his very soul felt suddenly a thrill he had never hitherto experienced. Beside him stood, in blushing modesty, a perfect child of nature— her dazzling black eyes flashing fire, under an excitement entirely new to her unsophisticated and primitive constitution—she felt abashed, yet knew not why—whilst Gaaham drank deep and largely at the first spring of love, and dwelt with rapture upon the perfect symmetry of her form, as she leaned against the huge trunk of the oak under which he had slept.

> "Her raven hair, half wreathed, descended,
> And o'er her face like shadows blended,
> Half veiling charms of fairer hue,
> Than ever forest daughter knew.
> Such looks ne'er decked the fairest child;—
> Ne'er bloomed such cheeks in forest wild."

Nathleocee possessed not only a face of loveliness, but a form, which might vie in beauty of proportion with the most exquisite productions of the Roman or Grecian sculptor.

Her costume was such as would shock the refined modesty of the more intellectual class of white females, but nature knows no shame but that of sin, and assuredly, if virtue consists in purity of thought, sentiment, or action—this artless girl was pure as the fountain which daily reflected her unrivalled charms.

The upper part of her form, according to the custom of her tribe, was left uncovered—her long black hair floated to the winds, unbraided, over her finely proportioned shoulders—and as the zephyrs caught the unconfined tresses, they would play upon a bust, Venus herself might have proudly owned. Her head was surmounted by a tuft of feathers, plucked from the wings of the snow-white Oartolo, or virgin crane; interspersed with those of the gaudy crimson flamingo—the whole confined by pearls of value, collected among the islands at the southern extremity of the peninsula of Florida.

She wore a skirt of chassee, or fawn's skin, of the softest texture, which was embroidered with minute sea shells, interspersed with pearls of rare beauty and extraordinary magnitude, and further ornamented with strips of ermine skins, and a variety of feathers of the richest hue. This Hukkasykee, as it is denominated in the

Seminole language, extended from her waist to a little below her knees.

Her beautifully formed legs were encased in Uphetaikas, also made of chassee, ornamented at the outsides by a double row of beads—a pair of prettily worked Mocassins, or Indian shoes, made to correspond with other portions of her dress, completed the attire of the Chieftain's niece.

Nathleocee was the orphan daughter of a neighbouring King, who had been killed in battle; from infancy she had been reared and cherished by her uncle, with all the fond affection which a noble-minded man feels for a lovely object looking up to him for protection. She was scarcely seventeen when Graham became enamoured of her extraordinary sylvan charms. With all the natural grace and dignity of one born free as the bounding fawn of the wilderness, she combined the retiring modesty, and feminine timidity of a girl just blushing into womanhood

—there was, withal, an arch playfulness, which caused the heart of many a young Seminole warrior to bound with rapture, when her piercing black eyes chanced to rest upon him.

Although she loved her "Hadke-tustenuggee," or white warrior, as Captain Graham was called throughout the Seminole nation, still she conceived it a degradation to be allied to an Iste-hadke, or white man; but at length yielded to his continued importunities, and they were married, according to the forms and ceremonies of the Seminole Indians.

Three successive seasons produced as many offspring to gladden the hearts of the affectionate parents—then came a withering blight upon their hopes of future happiness—the fond wife was destined to be separated by the rude hand of war, from her husband, and the father, from his children.

Hostilities were about to commence, and Graham was ordered by Oceola to quit the Indian dominions, with a threat, that should he again appear among them until the war with the whites had terminated, he would assuredly put him to death; it being customary on these occasions, for an Indian to sacrifice his dearest friend with his own hand, if found arrayed against the tribe to which he belongs. But, as a manifestation of his regard for his former friend and companion, on taking an affectionate leave of Graham, he pulled a white plume from his own head dress, and placed it in the military helmet of the young officer, telling him to wear it whenever he came into battle with the Seminoles, at the same time assuring him that he would give orders throughout the nation, that this insignia should be his protection!

The white warrior could not so easily control his affections, and in spite of the mandate of

Oceola, he again ventured into the vicinity of the wigwam which contained his wife and children. It was not long before an opportunity was afforded him of beholding her he loved. Nathleocee was on her way to visit the bank of a clear stream, beside which, under the shade of a wide-spreading magnolia, whose perfumes seemed like holy incense to their loves, the young couple had first exchanged their vows of pure affection.

No sooner had her keen eye discerned the tall, manly figure of her husband, than she prostrated herself upon the earth, hiding her beauteous face within her hands, and the most endearing entreaties could not extort from her a single word or look.

The rigid rules of obedience to her guardian, and honour to her tribe, forbade her to bestow upon Graham the smallest sign of love or recognition. Sooner would she have sacrificed her children and herself, than have gratified, by a single glance, the man who was sole lord of her affections.

Finding Nathleocee inexorable to all his impassioned entreaties, Graham left her to join his regiment; soon after which he was seen in the hottest of the fight at the battle of Ouithlacoochee, with the white plume waving in his helmet—but amidst such a shower of rifle balls and arrows, we are not surprised that he was unintentionally wounded, although not severely. Soon after this engagement he retired from the army, disdaining to draw his sword against a people he could not but love, and with whom he strongly sympathized, for their manifold wrongs and oppressions.

This unhappy princess, with her children, was subsequently taken prisoner, and confined in the fort of St. Augustine, while her husband was on a visit to his friends in New York.

From St. Augustine, this desolate family was removed, with other Indian captives, and transported to the "far west,"—there, probably, to perish, either by grief, change of climate, or starvation.

OF THE

PARENTS

OF

PRINCE ECONCHATTI.

"Hail, king! for so thou art."
SHAKSPERE.

ECONCHATTI-MICO.

Little more is known by white people of Econchatti, the father of the young prince, than that he was, previous to the war, King of the Red-hills, in the Seminole country; he does not appear ever to have much distinguished himself as a warrior; as at this time, so important to the interests of the Florida Indians, he gave up the command of his braves to his youthful and aspiring brother in law, Oceola; in this step manifesting much discernment and good sense—still it must be acknowledged, that with Indians, so much discretion and prudence prevail in war, that not much is known to their enemies of their government, either civil or military, until the Tomahawk is buried, and the Calumet of peace has been reciprocally smoked by both contending parties.

It seems, however, common enough among them for the command to be assumed, during war, by that chief who has had the greatest opportunities of signalizing himself, and who, in general, on the return of peace, retires to his post; resuming, with the rest of the young men, their habits of submission to the representatives of the families of the hereditary sovereigns; who, over the whole North American continent, are held in the greatest respect.

We are informed, by a copy of the correspondence between Horatio S. Dexter, Esq., agent for the Seminole Indians, and Captain Bell, of the United States army, and acting Governor of Florida, that as early as 1821, immediately after the cession of the territory from the Spanish government to the United States of America, Econchatti was then a King of a Seminole tribe; he is therefore always called Econchatti-Mico—the word mico signifying King or High chief. *Vide Appendix.*

At that time he resided with his sub-chiefs and warriors on the banks of the Chattahoochee river, where he possessed large private property, in land, slaves, horses, and horned cattle. At this place, it is presumed, the subject of the present narrative was born, who is nephew to the renowned Oceola—Econchatti having married Oceola's sister.

The wealth of Econchatti-Mico was a sufficient inducement for a party of neighbouring white ruffians to arm themselves, and without any previous declaration of hostilities, to rush suddenly into his dominions, when after killing one of his sub-chiefs, they forcibly took possession of the whole of his property. This may be considered as a trifling provocation on the part of the whites, but it is one only among thousands of a similar kind, which they have practised towards a people whom they stigmatize as "REVENGEFUL."

OF PRINCE ECONCHATTI'S MOTHER.

> " A death-like sleep,
> A gentle wafting to immortal life."
>
> MILTON.

A faint gleam of recollection of his mother at times flashes across the memory of this unsophisticated boy—he now brings to the vision of his mind the scene of her dying—and her death.

The loss of the maternal parent is in every grade of life more keenly felt in childhood's years, than that of the father; yet how much more poignant must have been the sorrow of this Indian child, whose hardy and stern sire, although possessing all the natural feelings of a parent or a husband, deems it unworthy his dignity to descend to the domestic cares of either; but whose stalwart arm is ever ready to defend her, the elect of his choice,—or his offspring—his only hope for future years—on whom he depends to convey to succeeding generations the fire and courage of his nature, and, perchance, through the same channel, by traditionary tales, to ages yet to come, the achievements of his heroic daring.

Sad and lonely then must have been the position of this young boy, whose mother breathed her last sigh in the wigwam, with no other attendant to administer to her dying wants than this feeble nurse of probably five years old. Cold was now that bosom on which he had lately nestled for warmth and comfort!

Oceola says that the death of his mother took place previous to the breaking out of the war;— he has not a clear remembrance of her, and the life he subsequently led was sufficient to replace the memory of his infantile years with more exciting events; he thinks his mother had been confined at home for some time—she had been bled in the temple, but the wound did not heal—his father came frequently, and sat with her, with which she was pleased; but on the morning of the day on which she died, he did not see his father as usual; probably he had gone away upon some military embassy, and as the other women were not present, it is not unlikely the families were already removed away into the interior of the country, to be more secure from the dangers of an impending war.

As soon as he observed his mother had ceased to breathe, he became frightened, and ran to the top of a hill; here he saw two Indians, who came immediately with him, and occupied themselves in examining carefully the extremities of a rope extended between two trees; they then went into the house, and he rambled away to a distance—on his return the men were gone, and the body of his mother was removed—he saw her no more. As he has no recollection of her in health, it is to be presumed she had been for some time an invalid.

The cord was doubtless designed to lash the body, being part of their ceremony in burial, which is thus performed. As soon as Indians are convinced of the death of one of their people, they place the arms close to the sides—the hands are bent up to the shoulders, and the knees are forced up to the chin.* In this position the body, after having been dressed in its best garments, is bound tightly round by a cord made of twisted strips of cattle-hide; it is then buried, if convenient, in some cavern, or it is carefully deposited in a hollow tree, and with it are placed

* There is a body of a South American Indian in the Museum of the College of Surgeons in London, discovered in this posture in the sand—erroneously supposed to have been buried alive by an earthquake.

all the ornaments, articles of war or dress belonging to the deceased—the places of sepulture are concealed, at times, with matchless skill.

The property of a deceased person is considered too sacred for the use of survivors—all their earthenware utensils, and other household property are broken up and destroyed, so that the ground in the vicinity of old Indian towns, is literally strewed with fragments of pottery, &c.

How revolting then to their notions, must be our disputes respecting the property of our dead friends, or the instances which more frequently come to their knowledge, of soldiers robbing the bodies of their own comrades, as well as of their enemies.

After a battle, the slain are collected in one spot, and a large mound of earth is heaped over them—some of these Indian mounds, as they are called, are very large; there is one I observed on the road from St. Augustine to Tomaka, which must have covered two acres of ground. *Barrows* of this kind are numerous over the whole American continent; showing a similarity of habits, in this respect, as well as in many others, between the Indians and the aborigines of Great Britain.

YAHCHILANEE and ALLAHA.

"Sounded at once the bow, and swiftly flies
The feather'd death, and hisses through the skies."
                                        DRYDEN.

Whilst upon the subject of Indian burials, I will take this opportunity of relating the ceremony, as more fully explained to me by the amiable daughter of Mr. Dexter, whose name is mentioned in the appendix—the young lady was witness to the rite she very pleasingly described. The unfortunate subject was a beautiful young Princess of the Euchee tribe, who previous to her marriage with a young sub-chief of the Seminoles, was absolutely persecuted by the addresses of a warrior of her own tribe—but the impassioned Euchee was rejected, and in the bitterness of jealousy, he swore revenge.

Eleven moons of uninterrupted happiness had glided rapidly away, and Allaha (the orange) had become the mother of a boy—the idol of his father, whom she loved with the devotion of woman's first and only love, and they were happy.

One evening as the fond mother was playing with her infant, which was suspended in a Wyya (a curiously constructed crib in which infants are placed, specimens of which may be seen in Catlin's exhibition) from a branch of a large oak tree—beneath which her husband was listlessly swinging in his grass hammock—an unknown Indian, who had been lurking throughout the day in a dense wood near by, was seen, just as the last rays of twilight died away, to rise from a mossy couch, and creep along in a half bent posture to the edge of the thicket near the

Wigwam, and in an instant the fond mother fell mortally wounded at the feet of her husband—an arrow had pierced her side, and before many minutes Allaha was a corpse.

The bold Yahchilanee, (war eagle) with a tearless eye, and a countenance expressive of the most intense anguish, leaned over his dying wife, uttering audibly at intervals "lepust, lepust!"—the breath is going, the breath is going! while an old crone of the tribe held the infant boy over the dying mother, to receive her parting spirit;—which is supposed to linger for a time with the offspring, and impart instructions which are to exert an influence upon its future destiny.

When it became evident that life was extinct, those around began to place the body in as compact a manner as possible, in the mode already described; it was then enveloped in a blanket and placed in a sitting posture.—The fire in and around the Wigwam was extinguished, and all blankets, utensils, ornaments, &c. were collected together—two Indians then passed a pole through the upper part of the blanket containing the body, and marched off to a distance followed by the husband and friends.

Having selected a place for encampment, fires were again kindled—and now commenced the ceremonies preliminary to burying the dead.—A feast was held for three days—the body placed in the open air handsomely attired, and a large fire encircled it, which was kept up until the expiration of the feast, when the body was removed for burial. As no such ready-made cemetery as a hollow tree was convenient, the friends proceeded to construct a mausoleum of young pine trees laid upon each other, forming a hollow square—of sufficient height to receive the body in a sitting posture—into which the remains of Allaha were deposited;

together with all her cooking utensils, bedding, beads, belts, and bracelets; besides a supply of poultry and provisions—and finally a little negress was decapitated and placed beside her mistress as an attendant across the Big-Prairie, until she should arrive in the hunting grounds of the GREAT SPIRIT. A few Indian girls, who had followed the train, plucked wild flowers, and strewed them around the corpse—fit emblems of her own fragile and short-lived existence!—Lastly, the tomb was covered with earth.

Now commenced the wailing and lamentation for the dead—tearing of hair, with every gesticulation of the agony of extreme sorrow: not so with the sad and silent mourner—the widower;—

> "No sigh nor moan escaped his quivering lips—
> But the look of woe unutterable—
> Extremity of earthly woe was there."

More than a year elapsed before the murderer fell under the knife of Yahchilanee—who never rested until satiated by the blood of the destroyer of his wife.

The Indian widower unbinds his hair, allowing it to float loose, and divests himself of every ornament for the space of three moons; during which time he appears sullen and gloomy, and enters on the chase only when the imperious demands of hunger impel him.

Of the private character of Econchatti-Mico, or of his wife, I have had no means of obtaining any intelligence beyond what little their child is able to communicate;—he remembers his father occasionally playing with, and caressing, him,—at times taking him on his knee, or carrying him on his back; and at night, in their open-air encampments, covering him with the same bear-skin. He can also recollect, that during the sickness of his mother, his father came frequently and sat with her; manifesting, as far as his young memory serves, the ordinary feelings of a father and a husband; which, I venture to state, are quite as strong, if not more so, among those denominated "savages," than among their destroyers, or even the really civilized Europeans.

I can by no means arrive at any certainty with respect to the death of Econchatti-Mico; it has been said that he was killed in battle, and again, that he died while a prisoner in the Fort of St. Augustine.

PRINCE ECONCHATTI FIRST CAPTURED.

"Thou hast, by tyranny, these many years,
Wasted our country, slain our citizens,
And sent our sons and husbands captive."

SHAKSPEARE.

This event could not long have preceded the second time when young Oceola was taken prisoner, as the Seminole war did not commence until November, 1835, and he was again in the hands of his enemies, in August the following year; thus making it evident that this persecuted child became twice a prisoner of war within the space of a few months.

In relating this circumstance, he can only recall to his memory that the Indians had halted in the Pine-forest for the night, and the following morning the *war-men* were obliged to leave their squaws and children to continue their journey unprotected, to their place of destination; they travelled alone for two or three days, when they were suddenly surrounded by soldiers on horseback, and taken prisoners.

The frantic mothers, with their children, were now driven, like a herd of cattle, to the nearest encampment of the Whites, and there placed upon baggage-waggons, to pursue their march towards the civilized districts of East Florida. They were several days travelling in this manner, sleeping at night under the broad face of Heaven, with a guard of soldiers placed over them.

On the road, Oceola saw many ruins of houses, recently destroyed by fire:—the whole district of country showed evidences of the devastating effect of war.

Rations of flour were issued for the Indian women and children, which they converted into cakes by placing them upon the coals of their fire. The young adventurer goes on to state that, whilst crossing a wide shallow stream, over which he was carried on the back of an Indian woman who had had the charge of him since the death of his mother, he observed a white man on the opposite bank making frequent threatening signs with a whip; menacing the women with a view to quell a sudden loud and garrulous impulse, which seemed to have seized them. They kept up constant noises and splashings in the water as they crossed, for the express purpose of being discovered by their friends, which the whites were, of course, anxious to prevent.

At length they arrived at the skirts of a village inhabited by white people, where they saw more soldiers: the prisoners bivouaced in the vicinity—the guard remaining at a short distance. During the night, two Indian women, a little girl, and Oceola, took advantage of an *unguarded moment*, and effected their escape under the mantle of darkness. They walked the whole of that night, and continued on their retreat for two or three days—resting occasionally in the dense hammocks, and subsisting during the time on *water melons* and *Indian corn*. They at last arrived at a place where they had encamped previous to their being captured;—here they had the good fortune to meet the *war-men*—with whom, they spent the night around a cheerful fire, regaling themselves plentifully till they had satisfied their hunger.

We may picture to ourselves the wildness of this scene—and who can do otherwise than sympathize with these people on the raptures of their reunion after their unexpected escape from captivity?—the result of which would, otherwise, have been either death or expatriation for many hundred miles, to a severe climate, and destined probably never again to meet those they held dear on earth.

It may be said, that human beings, in savage life, cannot possess in so high a degree, the enjoyments maintained by intellectual refinement; but, I contend they are more highly endued with the love of offspring than a great portion of civilized society.

Although an Indian woman has been known to stifle her child, that its cries might not betray a body of her people to an unsparing enemy, this apparently revolting and unnatural circumstance, does not detract from her feeling as a mother;—it appears to me an act of extraordinary heroism, evincing a power of mind, unknown since the days of ancient Sparta, or of Rome. Let me ask—would an Indian mother allow the fountain of life to the infant to dry up, and consign her child to the care of a stranger, that she might be the better enabled to revel in dissipation and luxury—or drown or strangle her offspring to hide her own shame?—Never!! Yet such occurrences are daily witnessed in *civilized* society.

FIGHT FOR A HOG.

"You have brought your hogs to a fine market."
SPECTATOR.

Oceola remembers an engagement with soldiers, when Econchatti-Mico, with a party of Indians, had halted near one of the military encampments of the whites—and one of his men made free to help himself to a hog belonging, it is presumed, to the enemy. As they were quartering the prize they were suddenly charged by cavalry, and a smart contest ensued, in which the soldiers were repulsed—leaving, for the use of their victorious foes all their horses, but taking away with them their wounded comrades.

At the onset, all the women and children hurried away as rapidly as possible. Oceola was so near the scene of action that he distinctly heard a musket ball pass across his breast, the sound of which he knew by its peculiar *zing*. The horses appear to have fallen into their hands very opportunely—the worn-out squaws, with their young ones, were forthwith mounted as well as the men;—Oceola's father, he observes, caught "a first-rate one," on which he rode away with his son *en croupe*.

ECONCHATTI-MICO WOUNDED.

"I am faint, my gashes cry for help."
SHAKSPERE.

Our young Prince states, that the day on which his father was wounded, and on the previous one, they had endured much fatigue; marching through thick swamps and the interminable pine forests—and the greater part of the preceding night had been spent in a retreat from their enemies.

We may here figure to ourselves the distress of these poor fugitives, keeping in view the party, consisting in a great measure of houseless women and children, who knew no refuge or shelter—frequently wanting fire and food, and chased by a merciless enemy, like herds of the wilderness, from one extremity to the other of a forest covering an area of fifty thousand miles.

Our youthful narrator speaks of his having been carried, on the back of his father, a great part of the way, until they halted towards evening in a dense thicket, so shaded that the sun could not penetrate.

The women and children were exhausted by the fatigues of the day's march, and now hoped for some respite from pain and toil—a cheerful fire was ignited, and they had begun to prepare refreshments of dried meat and Coontee—(a flour prepared from a wild root of the woods). In the midst of this miserable attempt to relieve the cravings of hunger, they were again surprised by an alarm—bloodhounds both biped and quadruped were again upon their tracks—

" Now all was hurry, and hot haste."

The blazing fire that seemed cheerfully to smile upon their afflictions, was speedily extinguished, and a few blankets which sometimes screened them from the fury of the elements, when suspended upon sticks, at others forming their only beds from damp and cold, were rapidly rolled up ready for a retreat. While the women were thus occupied, Nikkanochee remembers his father lifting him in his arms, that he might, even when so young, become accustomed to danger — he pointed out to him the steady approach of an enemy, whose muskets and bayonets gleamed in the brilliant golden hues of the setting sun.—After having stedfastly surveyed the phalanx of his foes, the boy was ordered by his father to rejoin the women and children, who had secreted themselves far in the tangled screens of the swampy hammock, while the warriors were left to defend them against the combined assaults of men and dogs; the latter Oceola describes as having been very annoying.—*Vide Appendix.*

The whites were repulsed with a loss of some killed and wounded. When this skirmish was ended and the soldiers had yielded to the Indians, the proud privilege their forefathers boasted—the right of possession of the land they lived on,—Oceola discovered his heroic father laying upon the earth, pale and faint from loss of blood—a musket ball had passed through his wrist; of this touching scene, the boy gave a clear description in the most artless garb of truth.

Far less secure were these unhappy fugitives than the wild beasts of the forest—the chase of which ceases with the declining orb of day; but the native Red man, the true, the hereditary lord of the soil, who never slays but in self-defence, or to avenge the death of a friend or relative—to whom God hath given dominion over the beasts of the field and forest to supply his wants—is persecuted, goaded, robbed, hunted, and at length destroyed, to make room for the innovations of civilized men; with whom, alas! too often, come rapine, debauchery, and "all the ills that flesh is heir to," in the walks of luxury and refinement.

After this action, in which Econchatti and several others were wounded, the Indians spent an anxious night in the hammock, and early in the morning, under dread of a reinforcement to the strength of their enemies, they again fled in search of safety for the women and children.

It starts the tear of pity to reflect upon the cruel persecutions of these unhappy people, in their struggle for freedom and their rights. They retreated through the dreary pine forests and muddy swamps and marshes, selecting those routes which would the most readily embarrass their pursuers. Oceola was at times carried upon the back of his father, who swam thus with his child over deep, broad, and rapid rivers, stemming the waters with one hand—at other times, he says, he was whipped by his uncle Oceola, for not walking fast enough to keep pace with the fugitive party.

After a weary march of two nights and a day, they again selected a resting-place near the edge of a hammock, and had kindled a cheerful fire—around which, some had stretched themselves, whilst others were occupied in preparing a repast of wild turkey and deer, which had, during their journey, yielded to that silent messenger of death—the arrow.

A short respite to their toils and troubles was allowed by their enemies. No sooner had they tasted the blessings of rest, with the comfort of a blazing fire-side, than they were once more startled by the plashing of horses, and the noise of soldiers crossing a river near their unsheltered encampment. The Indians now cautiously extinguished their fire, and remained quiet, until their foes had passed without having discovered them; they then renewed their fire and their fare—watching throughout the night in dread of an attack.

Oceola remembers that his father's arm was bound up, and placed in a sling, after the manner in use amongst us—which was still carried in a sling on the day of his own capture; on this occasion it was, that he saw his father for the last time.

The history of the young Prince now becomes peculiarly interesting. We have no right to expect much to excite our wonder, or even our admiration, in the adventures of a child, as dictated by himself, previous to the age of six years—but when we reflect, that the sufferings and privations of this poor boy, hunted like a fawn, must have endured through a war in which ten thousand disciplined troops, aided by ferocious BLOODHOUNDS, were continually upon the track of his persecuted tribe—not numbering two thousand warriors, whose almost only safety was in continued retreat through deep morasses, and almost impenetrable hammocks, or dense woods—bereft of their homes, and at times wanting the common sustenance of nature;—our warmest sympathies are roused in his behalf.

Not only are our feelings of commiseration confined to him, but they are widely diffused for the whole of his persecuted race.

The preceding pages show that a considerable portion of the life of this interesting child before his second captivity, formed a succession of events peculiarly harrassing; consequently we are not surprised that he appeared emaciated, feeble, and dejected, when he again fell into the hands of his enemies.

It is manifest to every reflecting mind that his steps were here directed by an all-wise Providence, who, in goodness and mercy, selected him from his unhappy tribe, to become, I trust, in future years, the means of conveying such information to his own people as may ultimately reconcile them to the new life they are undoubtedly destined to endure; for, there can be no scruple in saying, that these people, who once numbered upwards of a million, but now reduced to a few hundreds — must, ere long, submit to the dominion of stronger powers; however unjust the assumption of rights of conquest may be.

OCEOLA NIKKANOCHEE,

PRINCE OF ECONCHATTI, RECAPTURED.

"The tear down childhood's cheek that flows
Is like the dewdrop on the rose;—
When next the summer's breeze comes by,
And waves the bush—the flower is dry."

On the morning of the 26th of August, 1836, a little Indian Boy was brought a prisoner to Col. Warren, Commandant at the Military Station at Newnansville, having been captured on the preceding evening by soldiers, some miles from that place. The child seemed to be five or six years old; he was emaciated, and his general appearance indicated extreme suffering; he spoke not—and for at least three weeks he maintained nearly a perfect silence—he was apparently brooding over what he felt was a heavy misfortune, and was evidently well aware that he was in the hands of those whom he knew to be his enemies—he looked cautiously and quickly around him whenever a sound reached his ears.—The most trifling movement of those about him did not escape his notice—he manifested an extreme apprehension of danger, and it was thought that he was perpetually on the watch for an opportunity to escape.

Whatever passed in his infant brain, it was quite clear that he did not contemplate starvation, as he ate the bread and milk which was given him, accepting it however, with indifference or shyness, and again relapsing into his state of sadness when his meal was finished;—he was never heard to sob, cry, nor moan, but generally sat on the floor crosslegged—motionless and thoughtful, and appeared overwhelmed with a melancholy, which, in one so young, was touching to witness.

The report of his capture was as follows.—On the 25th of August, 1836, a scouting party of five soldiers set out from Newnansville to scour the surrounding country, and look out for signs of Indians. Early in the morning they disturbed several who were helping themselves to some sweet potatoes, in a fenced field belonging to a deserted residence: the Indians took the alarm time enough to leap over the fence and make their escape, retreating over a small stream into the forest, through which the soldiers followed the trails of one or two a short distance; they then deemed it prudent to return, not knowing the strength of the enemy, and again made their way into one of the military roads lately made in Florida, where they soon fell upon the tracks of footsteps of an Indian child, rendered distinct by rain which had recently fallen; these they determined to pursue, considering it tolerably certain that they would be led thereby to one of the encampments of the tribe.

The soldiers declared that they followed this child from the rising to the setting of the sun, and were convinced that they must have traversed a distance not less than forty miles.

It may seem incredible in this country that a child so young could possibly walk thus far in the time specified, yet I cannot for a moment doubt it; such a feat is by no means uncommon in Florida—little negroes of a similar age will often accompany their parents on foot from Jacksonville to St. Augustine, and reach the end of their journey in a day; these places are about the same distance from each other.

Towards nightfall they came in sight of the little wanderer, he having in fact lost his way. With that quickness of hearing which characterizes all creatures in a wild state, he seemed to be aware of the approach of his pursuers, for they saw him bounding like a fawn to seek the covert of the bushes, and there they found him concealed in the high grass.

On being seized he uttered a scream of terror, expecting instant death; but he soon smiled through his fast falling tears, and in an imploring attitude held up a peach in his little hand, which he seemed to offer as a ransom for his life! He was immediately placed on horseback behind one of the soldiers, and it was quite dark before they reached Newnansville, where he was taken in charge by one of them for the night, who fed the poor little famished prisoner with a bowl of milk, and gave him a blanket, in which he wrapped himself after the Indian fashion, and lying down before the fire was soon asleep.

I now feel ashamed to mention a fact which

will startle my readers—but were 1 not to do so, I should not only fail in doing justice to one of the soldiers, whose conduct on this occasion does him honour, but should leave a very incorrect impression, as to the nature of the warfare carried on against these hapless Indians, besides passing over a circumstance of great interest in the eventful life of the boy.

Will it be believed that a dispute arose among the soldiers, as to the propriety of at once destroying their little captive? the *majority* deeming it right to sacrifice every Indian, whether man, woman, or child! At length JAMES SHIELDS, to his renown be it mentioned, succeeded in preventing the perpetration of this horrid barbarity, and it is owing to his resolute interference, and to that alone, that the poor little fellow was brought into Newnansville ALIVE!!

Oh! ye happy parents of this highly enviable

country! compare the lot of your own blessed offspring, with that of this Indian Child—at an age which by you is considered one of nearly perfect enjoyment—when their little wants and wishes are studied and provided for with the most anxious solicitude—when nothing which can contribute to their health or welfare is for a moment neglected—when instructors begin to be provided, and the early buddings of intellect are watched for and observed with rapture indescribable—whose joy is your own, and who in fact constitute almost your second and dearer existences:—at the same age this Indian Child was a wanderer in a wild and desolate country, amidst interminable forests—beset by dangers —beyond the assistance of his father or kindred, and going he knew not whither!— But the hand of PROVIDENCE led him in safety through the wilderness, and we can now listen to his own artless and truthful tale of this eventful day of his early life.

Oceola well remembers the greater part of what happened to him when he was captured, and that only have I determined to write, and as nearly as possible in his own words.

PRINCE ECONCHATTI'S NARRATION.

He says that he, with his father and some more Indians were travelling, and came to a house which was deserted—in the garden belonging to which some sweet potatoes were growing: he had been carried on the back of a man, as were some other children, who let him down outside the fence, and then clambered with the other men into the "potatoe patch;" they had none of them, that he knew, tasted food that morning; he himself had not.

Almost immediately they were alarmed by soldiers, and the Indians quickly returned over the fence, when Oceola saw his father beckoning him to come on, but the white people came so quickly, that he was obliged to join the rest in their flight.

There was a rivulet which the Indians all leaped, and in endeavouring to follow them he partly gained the opposite bank, but fell back into it—he got up and reached the other side, when he tripped against a vine root and again fell; on getting up and running forward he could see none of his companions, except an old Indian, who did not appear to see him—they had all, according to their custom, dispersed in different directions.

It may appear to those unacquainted with Indian life, cruel for a father to abandon his child under such circumstances, at the risk of his falling into the hands of an unfeeling enemy; but Indian children are early taught the habits of all wild creatures, and in case of surprise know how to secrete themselves in the bushes or high grass, or in the hollow of a tree, and in places where few whites would suspect their being concealed; whilst the parents and warriors take measures for their own safety, and at the same time by attacking or drawing off their enemies from the place, secure that of their children. The child thus hidden lies as still as a partridge, till the danger being over, the father or mother repair to the spot, and by a peculiar call or cry, which is adopted by each family, he starts up and they become re-united.

The child continued his flight; he remembers passing an old house, and came into the road—he was not yet frightened, as he fancied he was following his people, in consequence of observing an old coffee-pot with something green in it placed on a log, and which he had seen in an Indian woman's hand in the early part of the day.—This is another of their means of directing stragglers in their flight—dropping unimportant articles, breaking down small twigs from the bushes as they pass, and pointing them in the proper direction, with many other signs, known only to themselves.

He continued along the road, and saw the tracks of baggage waggons and picked up a musket ball; after this he saw no signs of the way his people had gone, and then he says he "began not to like it much;" he soon after came in sight of a small village or settlement of the whites, whereupon he struck out of the road, and skulked along at some distance behind the bushes, so as to keep himself out of sight—the place, like all others in the neighbourhood, was deserted—he obtained the road again, and late in the afternoon came to another deserted house, adjoining which was a peach-orchard.

Having had no breakfast, nor eaten nor drunk during the whole day, he went in and satisfied his hunger with peaches; he took a few away with him, placing them in the front part of his dress. It was getting dusk when he left the peach-orchard, and had not gone far before he heard a noise — looking round him he saw soldiers at a distance; he then ran with all his might — the soldiers gallopped after him; he soon saw they were getting too near, therefore struck off the road, and hid himself in the grass; he saw some of the men come up and stop near his hiding-place, but one of them, it seems, had marked him, and rode directly to the place of his concealment, and calling out to the other men, leaped from his horse and took him by the arm. Oceola then began to cry, thinking he was going to be killed, at the same time he offered *one* of his peaches, hoping that might save his life.

The soldier took it and smiled, then returned it to him, and taking him up in his arms, mounted his horse and placed him behind him, and then they went on.

The men talked nearly all the way until they reached Newnansville, when it was quite dark—the soldiers took him to a house, and gave him a bowl of milk and a blanket, then went up stairs to bed; he drank the milk, feeling very hungry, and then wrapped himself up in the blanket before a good fire and went to sleep.

Although awake early on the following morning, he did not move till the soldier came down stairs, when he was taken by the hand and led into the guard-room· here he saw Col. Warren for the first time, who consigned him to the care of James Shields; at his house he had no food given to him until dinner time, when he had some bread and other food. Shields treated him with great kindness, and never trusted him out of his sight—he made him sleep on a little moss bed, in the same room with him.

For breakfast he had bread and butter, but the butter he disliked, and scraped it off with his fingers.

A day or two after his arrival in Newnansville, he witnessed the funerals of two soldiers; sights, which he unhesitatingly says gave him great pleasure. Child as he then was, he had already imbibed a strong hatred to all white people, but of course to soldiers in particular—the persecutors and slayers of his race!

In a few days he was elated by a discovery that the place was surrounded by Indians, when he felt great hopes of obtaining his deliverance, and restoration to his friends; he knew this by the noise and stir—by Col. Warren buckling on his sword, and the soldiers arming themselves; he did not know that any one was killed, he heard no guns fired, and thinks the Indians went away again without attempting anything.

It is not at all improbable that some of the Indians with their ordinary precaution, had, in their turn, tracked the soldiers and the child, until he was taken prisoner by them; and that the anxious father returned upon the back trail as far as Newnansville, and then, aided by an increased number of warriors, surrounded the place with the intention of effecting the young Prince's deliverance. But the poor boy's hopes were doomed to disappointment, for at this juncture, a reinforcement of troops arrived, and but just in time to save the whole garrison from the scalping knives of the outraged Seminoles; this, although he knew it not, was the cause of the dispersion of the Indians, without their making any attempt at his rescue.

It was well known to the officers in Newnansville that the Chief—Oceola—at the time commanded in person, and they now surmised that their prisoner was one of too important a character to be allowed to remain among them; consequently, soon after this event he was removed under a guard (but still in the immediate charge of James Shields) to the private residence of Col. Warren, at Jacksonville; a town many miles beyond the Indian frontier. Instead of sending Oceola a prisoner to head-quarters, Col. Warren, with commendable kindness and generosity, removed him with his family to his country residence, where he passed about a year, and here placed him with his own children, with whom he ate, drank, played, and slept. Although the child of their enemies, he soon engaged the affections and kindly feelings of the Colonel's whole establishment. It not unfrequently occurred, that when boyish dissensions arose, and complaints were brought to him by his own children of

I

the infringement of the young Indian on the rules of play, he would be but little inclined to take their part, but admonish them to be more kind and conciliatory to the little captive.

For the convenience of the reader I will now interrupt the thread of the narrative. The child is passing his time in an estimable family, where we will for the present leave him, and revert to the earlier part of his existence. Doubtless much curiosity is felt to know how he passed the first few years of infantile life, previous to his being taken prisoner, from the insight it may afford into the domestic habits of the Indians—what were his amusements, and those of other children of his tribe—his recollections of his parents and relations, and of events which took place during, what we call, "the happy days of childhood." This part of my undertaking must, however, for obvious reasons, be but imperfectly accomplished, but it shall be attempted.

PRINCE ECONCHATTI'S REMEMBRANCES OF HIS EARLY DAYS.

> "Sometimes forgotten things, long cast behind,
> Rush forward in the brain and come to mind."
>
> SHAKSPEARE.

It need hardly be said that the childish years of Oceola were passed not in the lap of comfort and security, but in an almost constant struggle with dangers and privations; or in endeavours to elude the pursuit of his white enemies; to effect which, his tribe was kept in a perpetual state of watchfulness.

Previous to this state of life, which commenced with the outbreaking of the war; his remembrances of the days he spent in the wilderness, must of course be very limited and unimportant; still we cannot but feel an interest in almost every circumstance connected with this child of a noble Chief—the ruler of a warlike people.

Before the epoch alluded to, he spent his days with other boys in rambles about the forest in the vicinity of his home. The older boys would avail themselves of the dark nights to go into the hammocks, with torches made of split resinous pine wood, to seek among the low branches of trees for the opossums, which when discovered, they knocked on the head with sticks—this, and the amusement of shooting the racoon by day with bows and arrows, afforded them much delight.

His ordinary food consisted of roasted turkey or meat, chiefly Echa or deer's flesh, and Saufkee or Indian corn bruised in a mortar and boiled, called by the Americans homminy. The mortar was a block of wood hollowed out; the pestle of which was formed of a piece of hard wood about three feet long, heavy and large at each end—the pot in which the food was cooked was made of clay, shaped by the hand and dried in the sun, and then baked in the fire; these utensils are always ornamented with indentations and marks. They eat their food out of gourds with wooden spoons. Sometimes squirrels were skinned and roasted, at other times they were rolled and tied up like a ball and put into the ashes, and skinned when they were sufficiently cooked. Their thirst was generally quenched at the limpid stream, in large leaves, so twisted as to make a cup.

When not encamped, or in a house, Oceola usually slept on the ground, under trees in the woods; generally with some kind of covering, as a deer-skin, bear-skin, or blanket.

He was once, by some accidental circumstance, lost in the woods, and after rambling nearly the whole day in search of his father's encampment, he saw at a distance the smoke curling above the trees; even this cheering sight did not induce him to run at once to the spot from whence it came, but he cautiously reconnoitred about until he heard his own tongue, and felt well assured he had not mistaken the camp of an enemy for his own. He found his friends engaged over their evening meal, consisting of a dish of fried potatoes, in which he partook with the avidity of a boy who had fasted the whole day.

MASK DANCE.

The only juvenile sports of which he has a clear recollection, and which he witnessed when too young to join in them, are the Ball-play (described in another chapter) and one called the "Mask Dance:"—his recital of the latter amusing ceremony, is distinct enough to enable him to give a tolerable description of it.

It is begun by the smaller boys, whose faces are covered with masks made of the bark of the cypress tree, in which holes are cut for them to see through; these grotesque screens to their merry faces, are raised high above the head, but do not descend below the chin.

The children becoming thoroughly enlivened

by dancing round a fire—the *war-men*, as Oceola always terms the fighting characters, and larger boys approach, with their faces also covered in the same manner—they seat themselves at a distance and watch the antics of the juveniles, till they themselves are constrained to join the boys and much fun ensues.—Here may be witnessed the noble warrior, like the famous Roman emperor Aurelius, throwing off his dignity, and happy in partaking the amusements of his children—here is the wild Indian—the lordly nobleman of nature, rioting in the affectionate feelings of a father, and relaxing his distant bearing and dignified demeanour; the remainder of the tribe sitting round, spectators of a scene, which, from associations or incidents unknown to us, doubtless affords all parties the highest enjoyment; inasmuch as these festivities commencing as darkness sets in, do not finish till day-break.

In the midst of this joyous assemblage rushes on a sudden from the bushes, a man terrifically decorated, holding in his hand a branch of some weed—an immediate yell of pretended alarm breaks forth from the athletic adults, and the really dismayed youngsters scamper off in every direction.

The phantom of the forest jumping through the fire, seizes any boy whom he can catch, and tickles him till his mask falls off; after leaping a few times through the fire, he retires to the bushes. The boys return, and each by dancing, and dreading a renewal of the tickling, is excited to the highest pitch of wariness and activity, increased by the apprehension of the reappearance of the "*Hulwagus.*" When a few more of the youths have been caught and unmasked their part is finished, and the dances of the war-men succeed, and Hulwagus continues to play his pranks among them.

Those of the tribe who choose to continue, witness displays of personal strength on the part of the youthful warriors, to which the gymnastic exercises of ancient Greece were mere child's play; the festival concludes by a substantial *breakfast* of roasted venison.

This sport seems calculated to harden the nerves of the young Indians, and to accustom them to sudden surprises from their enemies; in which the tactics of Indian warfare chiefly consist.

These and other amusements suited to childhood, were however but rarely indulged in after the war began—the fatigue consequent upon a hard day's march, in which the children were compelled to partake, though often carried upon the backs of their parents, inclined them to little else than to food and sleep. An ingenious and rational operation was usually performed, when the long travel of the day was likely to occasion stiffness, and thus impede their journey on the succeeding one; to this operation, when thought requisite, both old and young were compelled to submit. Oceola has often undergone it, and says he did not think it very painful; it consists in scarifying the legs and ankles with sharp fish-bones, till the blood flows in sufficient quantity to afford relief, and to prevent both swelling and stiffness—it seems to be an established custom, and is doubtless an effectual one.

On the return of Colonel Warren with his family to Jacksonville, the little Indian accompanied them, and again became my frequent visitor; the interest I had previouly felt for him was revived with increased force. He had now acquired a sufficient knowledge of English to make himself tolerably well understood; his health had greatly improved, and he had grown a pretty and interesting child: although he had become communicative with his young companions, he was, with older persons, still shy and reserved; and no one had yet succeeded in eliciting from him his own name, or that of his parents; or could induce him to say anything relating to his family or tribe—subjects on which he was always silent. Entertaining, as my reader has already been informed, a strong feeling of regard for the Indian character, my sympathies for the little captive became daily more strongly excited; as I fancied I observed in him the dawning of the good qualities peculiar to his race; and reflected, that notwithstanding the kind treatment he now received, he would eventually be claimed as a prisoner of war, and undergo the fate which many of his exiled tribe had already suffered.

His peculiar situation at length determined me, if possible, to constitute myself his guardian; and Colonel Warren being on the point of making an important change in his own family, gave me an opportunity of preferring my request: it was willingly granted, and this friendless child accordingly came under my immediate protection on the 31st of October, 1837.

This change, separating him from his young companions, caused him to relapse into his former taciturnity, observable in him when he was first captured—his fear of strangers was very great, and of the white country people, or *Crackers*, as they are there called, he had a particular dread; no sooner did he apprehend their arrival than he instantly flew to some place of concealment.

That he should have displayed such an aversion cannot be wondered at, as he knew they had frequently expressed a threat to kill him the first opportunity that offered with safety to themselves; among whom the destruction of an Indian, however small, would have been a satisfactory achievement.

I now sent him to a school, with the children of several respectable families in the neighbourhood, kept by a lady of conciliatory manners and superior understanding. For several days no perceptible change took place; he returned home regularly, and would quietly squat himself on the floor by the side of his adopted mother, not noticing any kind greeting or marked attention. He would join the family at meals, signifying his acceptance of what was offered by a nod of his head—a shake of which denoted his refusal. He gave a marked preference to vegetable and farinaceous food of the simplest kind, and objected to all stimulating condiments. Malt liquor, wine, and spirits he decidedly refused, but of lemonade or sweetened water he partook freely—on sweets in general he delighted to feast abundantly.

It was truly pleasing to watch the early buddings of his infant mind, and to observe his gradual approach towards the habits of civilized life. At night he willingly came to the side of his foster-parent, who taught him on his knees, to offer up his first prayer to his Heavenly Father. It was long before he could repeat by heart the LORD's PRAYER—but seemed desirous to please in his efforts to pronounce the words clearly and with precision.

Miss D—— was earnestly requested to exert the influence she maintained as governess, to learn from the child the names of himself and family, in which she succeeded as far as that of himself and his father—he whispered his own name with extreme caution—it was Nikkanochee. When he divulged this first secret, he looked round timidly to discover if any one noticed him—Miss D—— immediately committed it to paper, and without his cognizance handed it to my wife.

Elated with her success, she urged him to disclose the name of his father. To show the extraordinary discretion of one so young, he now tells me he gave her, and others, the name of *another* Indian, that his father might not be discovered, and it was some time after this that he told us who his father really was, which we then understood to be Conchatti.

His reserve gradually abated, and by degrees he made known to us a portion of his early history. Among other subjects of inquiry, I will name one which threw further light upon his family connections. He came home one day from school in tears; and complained that Miss D—— had whipped him, and on being asked if he had ever been whipped whilst with his tribe, he replied " Yes;"—his uncle had once punished him with small switches to make him walk faster, when probably retreating from their enemies, and on being questioned what was the name of his uncle, in an instant he answered Oceola.

The relationship between Oceola and his father was afterwards satisfactorily explained to me by Captain John Graham, of the United States army; who lived several years on the Indian frontier, and was intimate with Oceola, whose niece he married, and by whom he had a family. Dining at the house of Judge Reid at St. Augustine, who is now governor of Florida, on the 1st of August, 1838, a conversation was started between Mrs. Reid and myself respecting the little Indian boy, with regard to whom she had always manifested a warm interest; some pleasant bantering ensued on my venturing to express a supposition that he was nephew of the great Oceola: Captain Graham, who was present, inquired the name of the boy's father, a lady having jokingly remarked that the child must be, also, a relation of his. I told him that his father's name was Conchatti; when to the surprise of Mrs. Reid, and my own peculiar gratification, he said that Econchatti, (or as he was more generally called, *Econchatti-Mico*,) married the sister of Oceola, and that consequently the boy's statement must be correct. All were now convinced that the little Indian was in reality the nephew of Oceola.

This information was subsequently confirmed by Dr. Simmons of St. Augustine, than whom perhaps no man in Florida is better informed in all relating to the Seminoles and their language: he was well acquainted both with Oceola and Econchatti, and explained to me the meaning of the name of the latter.

Econchatti-Mico, he informed me, was his official name; that he was always thus called by his tribe in their "talk" with the whites; his name being thus written in all treaties made between them and the Indians; extracts from some of these documents proving which, will be found in the Appendix. That he was king of a tribe of Indians inhabiting a district of country called the "Red Hills," as his name implies— "Econ," meaning hill or hills—Chatti, red— Mico or Micco, King.

After staying at the town of Jacksonville about a year, I purchased an estate near the mouth of the St. John's river, to which with my *protegée* I removed, and there we remained until May 31st, 1840. Here he had full opportunities of indulging his taste for the wilder accomplishments of hunting and fishing, preferring then, naturally enough, to all else we endeavoured to teach him. His courage was remarkable; undauntedly he would climb the highest trees to rouse the racoon from his lair of sticks and dried leaves, and soon became perfect in loading a double-barrelled gun, which he as readily fired when permitted to do so.

At this time, he was supposed to be not more than eight years of age, but, on every occasion manifested the hardihood and freedom from fear peculiar to his race. At one time, I watched both with pleasure and anxiety his manœuvres with an alligator not less than twelve feet long, with which he was playfully amusing himself: he had thrown aside his dress, as was his custom in hot weather, whilst fishing on the bank of the St John's river. The huge amphibious monster moved stealthily along at the water's edge, and the boy would now and then wait within a few feet of his greedy foe— and as it advanced he would feign fear and retreat a few paces; then again watch quietly the approach of the hideous creature, poising a small spear which he always carried with him when seeking for fish. At length, knowing the habits of these animals, I perceived the alligator in right earnest preparing for his deadly attack; I therefore sprang forward and saved the boy from the impending danger; my presence alarmed the alligator, when, without making a ripple on the surface, it sank to the bottom of the river.

I interrogated the boy as to his intentions had the alligator molested him; he replied with perfect confidence and unconcern, "*I would have hit him right in the eye,*" suiting with his spear, the action to the word. This weapon he would use with wonderful precision and skill. The eyes of soles, when their bodies are covered by mud, are visible to none but a keen and practised observer: these fish I have seen him strike accurately with his spear, and raise them triumphantly in the air.

In reference to the alligators' mode of attack, I may mention that on shore they sometimes attempt to seize with the mouth, but more generally trip up their prey with the tail; the victim is then dragged into the water and held beneath by the mouth alone until dead; it is afterwards devoured ashore. A hearty meal lasts them for several days; and previous to burying themselves in the mud for the winter months, they swallow a large piece of wood, or some other hard substance, to keep the stomach distended until the following spring.

Oceola soon became an expert swimmer, and could paddle my small canoe with great dexterity. His endurance of fatigue in the woods was surprising; often when loitering after a walk of about twenty miles, he has laughed at my weariness, whilst he himself was fresh and active.

ANECDOTES AND PECULIARITIES OF INDIANS.

It is generally believed that Indians are not easily roused from their dignified and serious deportment, unless excited by anger; and that they are not readily fascinated by the charms of woman; but if the following be a correct statement, of which there can be no doubt, as the scene was witnessed by hundreds—then I say, they are susceptible in an eminent degree of the witchery of female beauty, heightened by the powers of dramatic art. In this instance at least, their gallantry could not be surpassed by the most refined gentleman in Europe.

A SCENE at the THEATRE in WASHINGTON.

FROM AN AMERICAN PAPER.

It was a novel and exciting spectacle at the Theatre, on the occasion of Miss Nelson's benefit. The boxes and the parquette were filled. On the left of the stage sat a delegation of Indian Chiefs, representing the Sioux, Ioways, Sacs, and Foxes, of the Missouri river. With a single exception, not one of them had ever before visited the settlements of his white brethren. Before them, in the parquette, they beheld a crowd of civilized men, mingled with whom were the kindred of some of them, the Sioux from the Falls of St. Anthony; part of these dressed in the military coats, with epaulettes, and hats, with silver bands, and others in the new blankets and leggings they had that day received as a present from their Great Father*—In the boxes was an array of females, looking with strange interest on these sons of the forest. But the attraction for the party on the left of the stage was the agile and fairy figure of the Mountain Sylph. As she descended, and her feet touched lightly the stage, their cries mingled with the plaudits of their white brethren. As she moved from place to place, appearing and vanishing with a rapidity that reminded them of the fleetness of the deer in their native hunting grounds, their interest became more intense. One of them, Pa-la-ne-a-pa-pi (the man struck by a Rickaree) a young chief of the Yanctons, suddenly rose, and threw at her feet the splendid war-cap, composed of feathers of the war-eagle, which he had often worn in bloody conflicts with the

* The President.

enemies of his people. Most gracefully did the Sylph receive the offering, and appended it to her own rich costume.

A few moments passed, and an aged Sac Chief, Po-ko-na (the plume) who, during a long life has been distinguished for his friendship, for the Americans, especially in the war of 1812, moved by a sudden impulse, made to her an oblation of his own war-cap. To-ka-ca (the man that inflicted the first wound) a celebrated brave of the Yanctons, almost immediately afterwards presented her with a splendid robe of the skins of the white wolf, which he had worn only at the more imposing ceremonies of his tribe. A buffalo robe, richly ornamented, was next the gift of Ha-sa-za (the forked horn) the second chief of the Yanctons. And Mou-ka-ush-ka, (the trembling earth) a young brave of rank, of the same tribe, bestowed another robe, of similar fabric and workmanship. At the presentation of his gift, each of these Chiefs and warriors addressed to the Sylph some words of compliment; the last declaring that he made his offering "to the Beauty of Washington." With grateful ease she expressed her regret that she could not speak to them in their native language, and thank them for their splendid donations; and she requested the interpreter to tell them that she should ever regard them as friends and brethren. Then, advancing to the box, she presented to each a beautiful ostrich plume, which they immediately placed upon their head-dresses. At the close, as she was ascending, she spread over her brow the splendid war-cap of eagle feathers, producing a most magical effect.

It would be vain to attempt to convey to those who were not present, an idea of the impression created by such an unwonted and unexpected exhibition of interest and admiration by these untutored men, who, for the first time, witnessed what they must have deemed a more than human exhibition of power. And well may the sylph felicitate herself upon having kindled so vividly their susceptibilities, and obtained from them such costly tokens of their admiration.

INDIAN DOCTORS IN FLORIDA.

The practice of the Seminole "Faculty," is confined exclusively to roots and herbs — of which an endless variety abound in the pine-woods and swamps of Florida. Steaming, and bleeding, also enter largely into their *modus operandi.*—The former is effected by the steam of water, in which herbs have been boiled; the patient, after having undergone this operation, is well soused with cold water. Phlebotomy is performed by a piece of broken glass bottle or a fish bone. Enchanted water is another remedy used by this superstitious people — a small quantity from some limpid spring is placed in a gourd, and a particular kind of root chipped into it; the doctor then blows upon it, uttering some unintelligible words, when the *holy water* is fit for use.

When an individual of the tribe is taken sick, and has called in medical aid, the doctor never leaves the patient until a change for the better is observed, or the spirit departs for the unknown land of the dead. He is perfectly devoted to the invalid, administering all his potions with his own hands — and, that the friends may not suspect him of mal-practice in case of death, he himself takes a dose similar to the one administered — no matter how often, or how nauseous it be — he swigs it down each time he prescribes for his patient; and if his applications do not effect a cure, no charge is made.

If the Legislatures of all civilized communities would enact a law to the same effect in relation to doctors — *id est*, to take their own potions as often as they administered them, many valuable lives might be spared.

AMUSEMENTS.

Dancing is, with the Seminoles, as it is with all wild nations, a favorite amusement;—no undertaking of importance can be commenced or terminated by them without a dance. Dancing comprises a part of their religious devotions—the sprightly time of marriage—hailing the new-born child—to the more solemn ceremony of death;—preparing for battle—or the execution of a prisoner or a criminal;—the first fruit-offering to the Great Spirit—going to, and returning from the chase—all are attended by a dance!

The names of some of their dances sound unmusical and harsh to ears refined; as, the

Wolf—the Bear—the Panther—Alligator, &c. Of all their dances, the War dance, and the Green-Corn dance, are the most imposing and amusing.

In performing those named after different objects of the chase, they dress themselves in the skins of the creature they wish to represent, carefully covering their own head with that part of the skin—they then commence by imitating the movements, *rampant et couchant* — with bellowing, roaring, or growling, as the case requires—dancing round in a circle—their feet keeping time to any of the aforesaid accompaniments, aided by a sort of tambourine, beaten with a stick.

This movement requires a great deal of muscular exertion, and is continued, without intermission, for a long time—probably half the same kind of exertion would completely prostrate the strength of the most athletic white man.

At the conclusion of the dance a loud whooping is commenced, and they generally break away upon a run in pursuit of one another.

THE WAR DANCE.—This ceremony is strictly prohibited in times of peace, and is punishable by death, unless consent of the King be obtained. —Many travellers in Florida have pretended to give a description of the War dance, but I have the authority of the oldest residents in the country who have lived years with the Seminoles, and who spoke their language fluently—that they never, although at frequent entreaties, could induce them to perform it; and I, myself, have repeatedly urged individual Indians to favor me with the war-whoop, but could never succeed during peace; but, after the commencement of hostilities, they were liberal to an unpleasant degree, without the ceremony of being "called upon."

Mr. Catlin, in his '*Tableaux Vivants Indiennes*,' gives a most animated, and, I have no doubt, a correct representation of this thrilling ceremony. —He lived eight years among the wildest tribes, who were at war with each other; consequently, where a white man had probably never before been seen, he was considered neutral, or identified with the party he happened to be residing with; therefore, he has had better opportunities of witnessing the War-dance, and their other ceremonies, than any other white man. As any attempt I might make to convey a comprehension of this *fête* could not possibly approach near to reality, I strongly urge my reader to visit the Egyptian Hall, where there is much to gratify the curious —both in the representations and costumes— and also in the splendid collection of Indian curiosities and paintings.

THE GREEN-CORN DANCE—is an annual festival; it occurs at the return of every season, when the maize or Indian corn has so far advanced as to be fit for boiling or roasting, which is probably a month or six weeks before it is thoroughly *hard ripe*. At this time, the whole nation meet at one particular spot for a grand and joyous *fête* — and to which, in times of peace, the pale-faced neighbours are invited.

This festival is supposed by many to have some analogy with the purification of the ancient Jews. It seems here to have for its design, purification as much as any other object—for the ceremonies anterior to the dance commence by medicine and bleeding. A large vessel of medicated liquid, called *the black drink*, is prepared, of which every individual of the tribes (for all are present) is compelled to partake—no one is exempt—no apology received—all must swallow it down, until they sicken and reel under its nauseating influence.

It is a powerful cathartic, which cleanses the system, and is supposed to be a promoter of health for the ensuing year. During this operation, blood-letting is also performed, as if to expel everything detrimental from the system; after which, ablutions complete the cleansing part of the ceremony. During this time all fires are extinguished—and now commences the offering to the GREAT SPIRIT: a fresh fire is produced by rubbing together two pieces of wood, which is attended with great exertion before ignition is effected; then a large pot, filled with green corn, is placed upon the fire—this is then burnt as an offering; after which, commences the boiling and roasting for the company.

There can be no doubt that the reason why Indians take the "black drink" is, that they think the system requires this annual refreshment—and, by way of enforcing this opinion upon the tribes, their doctors, magicians, or lawgivers—for all these professions are exercised by the same individual, have converted it into a religious ceremony.

Another design is, to make these days of rejoicing, that the seasons again give promise of being fruitful—that the FATHER OF BREATH has smiled upon the fruits of the earth, and that the genial influence of his servant, the Sun, is hastening them on to perfection. This is their rude way of offering the tribute of grateful hearts for HIS beneficence, and invoking HIS aid and blessing on the future.

During these days of hilarity there is an interchange of good feeling, and the cultivation of social affections among themselves; the lines of distinction among the various tribes, which are at all other times strictly observed, are here merged, and they meet and mingle like a band of brothers. On this occasion, if any one, who, during the past year, has committed a crime— no matter how heinous, unless it be murder— can contrive to skulk unobserved into the ring, while the ceremony is going on, no questions are asked, and he is at once restored to his former rank, and begins the new era as much respected as any of his tribe.

There is no Indian ceremony that tends so much to soften their stern nature as the Green-Corn dance. The young Sanhops or Braves, with their squaws, enter heart and soul into the sports of the time—while the old warriors, with their wives, look on in placid enjoyment—and when any great feat of agility is performed, they signify their admiration by grunting out, "Matto, matto!"—which ejaculation is commonly used to express thanks—it seems equally applicable to praise.

The Green-Corn festivals are also attended by games of ball. The BALL PLAY is performed by the young men, with a kind of spoon with a long handle, the bowl of which is coarsely wickered—the ball is thrown and caught in these instruments with much dexterity. *Football* is also a favorite amusement.

During this time the greatest good feeling exists—no bickerings or jealousy are allowed to manifest themselves—all join in applauding the warrior who performs the most distinguished feats. The young men here, as in the days of chivalry, glory in their achievements; each enjoys a conviction that his " ladye love" is made proud by his distinction — and thinks himself amply repaid for his laborious exertions by the melting glances of her dark eye. Like the Grecian games, they too serve to develop and strengthen the frame, and render the warrior better able to endure the fatigues of the chase, and the toils of war.

This festival strongly resembles one that was held among the natives of Mexico, as described by Salis, the Spanish historian, who accompanied the expedition of Cortez to the conquest of that country.—The rite described by him, however, was purely a religious one, mingled with a thousand barbarous and superstitious ceremonies. All was performed in a square, at the foot of an immense Temple in the great City of Tenuchtitlan — at which time human victims were sacrificed to the Sun.

The Temple was dedicated to the Sun, and its principal front was towards the east. One large room in this huge building was occupied by the High Priest, around the walls of whose apartment were suspended upon strings—the *skulls* of all who had been dedicated to the great luminary of day.

It would be an interesting task for the inquisitive scholar to trace out the analogy between the customs of these two species of a common race of people, and their origin, back to the ancient Jews (if from them they originate), and to examine into the causes which have operated to produce the several changes in a common custom—and, finally, to modify it from a barbarous rite into a useful and joyous festival.

ETIQUETTE.

In conversation the Indians never interrupt each other; those who are listening incline their heads, and look upon the ground in an attitude of attention. When one has finished his discourse, he who replies says 'che! mar ma watster,' meaning very well, and he then commences, the other listening with the same polite attention.

The squaws generally, with the exception of the wives of the chiefs, perform all the drudgery. In travelling with their Papooses (children), they carry them in a Wyya, suspended at the back by a broad strap across the forehead. On the top of this convenient contrivance is sometimes placed a heavy load, surmounted by another child astride, holding on to the hair of the mother's head.

If the husband and wife hunt in company, which they sometimes do—the spouse is loaded first, and sent home—and when the men hunt alone, the fruit of the chase is carried home, and thrown down at the door of the wigwam—the hostess then performs all the sundry offices of skinning, cleaning, and cooking.

When an Indian from a neighbouring tribe makes a visit, he calls upon no particular individual, no matter how extensive his acquaintance may be—he marches directly to the council house, and seats himself upon a skin on the floor (from which he never rises with the assistance of hands, but by an easy spring he gracefully erects himself); any one seeing him, carries the intelligence to the chief of a stranger's arrival, who repairs thither, and seats himself by the side of his guest—not a word or look is exchanged until food is brought; then, after refreshment, conversation commences, which is never of a scandalous nature. If an Indian thinks himself, or his family, or his friend, injured by another, he disdains to speak of it to a stranger, if he does not resent it himself.

THE SEMINOLES' OPINION OF THE ORIGIN OF THE HUMAN RACES.

They believe that the GREAT MASTER OF BREATH, at the creation of the world, formed three men — the Red, the White, and the Black; that he also made, at the same time, three things which were not in existence before, and enclosed them in three separate packages, the contents of which were unknown to the men, and laid them before them to choose. The Red Man, being the favorite of the GREAT SPIRIT, was allowed to make the first selection, and on opening his package, he found it to contain a bow, and quiver filled with arrows.

The White Man came next, and on examining his, found paper and quills.

The Negro came last; his package contained an axe and hoe. This is a tradition had from their fathers, who believed the packages emblematical of the future destinies of the races. As for the Mulattoes, they are considered not entitled to country or occupation, and are regarded as the meanest of God's creation.

When the delegates of this tribe waited upon the secretary of state, some years since, at Washington, an offer was made to establish schools among them. Econchatti-Mico said *"No! The bow and arrows were given to our people by the* FATHER OF LIFE. *Our bows are like his bow, and our arrows are like lightning, which strike with death—they give us food, and they kill our enemies. He sent you paper and quills, to mark down all that passes on earth—we hope you will mark the truth upon a straight line. No! we want no schools—my people are content with the bows and arrows."*

LAWS.

Their code of unwritten laws is simple, and adapted to their primitive state of society. It resembles, in many respects, that of the ancient Jews. Life for life—an eye for an eye—a tooth for a tooth.

When uncontaminated by civilized man, faith and good fellowship prevail among them, and but few excesses are committed. Polygamy is allowed, but few avail themselves of it, excepting the opulent chiefs. No Indian is allowed to marry, unless he has already evinced industry, and ability to support a family. Chastity, among them, is a prevailing virtue—its opposite is extremely rare.

The want of fidelity in either sex is punished

with severity—more particularly as regards the women. The frail one, for the first offence, is severely beaten, and then has her ears cut off with an old jagged knife— for the second offence, the nose is sacrificed—for the third, the upper lip is cut away—and for the fourth (which, of course, seldom happens), death.

This is an injury the men never forgive— revenge burns unceasingly in their bosoms, until the blood of the offender has washed away the stain. The males, when injured, take upon themselves the administration of justice.

A gentleman who resided upon the bank of the river St. John, at the time of the Treaty of Moultrie (1823), invited the Chiefs on their return from the *Talk* to dine with him. All things in readiness, the dinner was announced, when the guests marched in, in a lordly manner, according to rank, following the gentleman of the house. Each was shown to a seat, which all immediately occupied—excepting a young Chief who had never before dined at the table of a white man—he commenced removing all the dishes to the centre of the table, and then leaped with delight upon the festive board, and seated himself cross-legged before his new arrange ment, anticipating, no doubt, a glorious regale. The other guests, perceiving this unrefined movement, one and all cried out "Hilah, hilah, hilah!" then dragged him from his ungainly position. Order and quiet were soon restored, and the consumption of food was proceeding with as much despatch as may be imagined, considering the unvitiated state of their digestive organs; when another Indian arrived accompanied by a squaw.

The lady of the house introduced the newly-arrived guest, and his better half, into the dining hall; the Indian lady manifested the greatest reluctance at entering the room, as the

M

squaws never take their meals with their husbands. The interpreter explained the cause of her reluctance—he was requested by the white lady to tell Econchatti-Mico that they were ungallant, and should allow their wives to eat at the same table; and begged him to order his people to make room for the squaw and herself —the interpreter did as he was desired. The Chief was silent, the other Indians laughed, but no one moved. The hostess then walked up to the table, and pushing some of the Indians aside, made room for herself and the squaw, and both sat down at the table; at this the whole party burst into a loud laugh. The lady proceeded to help her guest, and urged her to eat, but in vain: at length, finding their custom a fixed one, she left the table. The squaw seemed abashed, and even distressed, by the awkwardness of her situation. Indian women always eat after the men, but they are generally near to perform such offices as cooling the food by fanning, and brushing off the flies.

INDIAN MARY.—One of the most touching illustrations of Indian kindness and sympathy for the whites, was exhibited in the case of poor Indian Mary, who was well known to all the planters on the St. John's River.

Mary, in her early days, had lived much among white families; she was remarkable for a bluntness of manners, which, to a stranger, appeared disrespectful. This peculiarity was by no means improved by the expression of a countenance decidedly ugly—her vision was very imperfect, from cataracts in both eyes, and as objects could strike the sight only in an oblique direction, when she was spoken to, her face was turned on one side—and her eyes, to catch the figure of the speaker, were considerably distorted from their natural position, producing a horrible squint — indeed, the expression of Mary's face was anything but prepossessing, and her person was altogether as forbidding as her countenance.

Yet, with all these ungainly attributes, Mary had an Indian husband—a man of no inconsiderable influence among the tribe, and by whom the race was augmented in numbers to the amount of five: she, with her husband and children, were frequently at my house, before the breaking out of hostilities; and at a time when I had not the remotest suspicion of the stirring scenes that so speedily ensued, in which the husband acted a conspicuous part.

This warrior, named Yaha-Ematkla-Chupka (leading Wolf), was a Sub-Chief, about thirty years of years; he usually wore a sort of frock, trimmed at the edges with a border of white cotton, confined to his body by a broad girdle handsomely ornamented with beads, in which was conspicuously seen a terrific-looking Saphka or scalping-knife—its handle was curiously ornamented; in front of him was suspended a beautifully-beaded Itcha-y-sucha or pouch, in which he carried his flints, balls, tobacco, and other little useful articles;—at his left side hung his carved powder-horn, and on his shoulder was placed his rifle. His neck was encircled by several strings of beads and silver crescents —from his ears hung minute sea-shells. His head-dress was of green cloth, the lower part of which was thickly studded with beads, and on the left side was gracefully placed several eagle feathers—his nether extremities were enveloped in leather buskins, and his feet shrouded in mocassins.

The countenance of Yaha-Ematkla-Chupka was harsh : but to analyze each feature, I should be disposed to pronounce his face handsome; a high intellectual forehead—a glancing, penetrating, jet black eye—nose perfectly Grecian—

mouth small, but lips too large to be in keeping with the symmetry of his other features—a chin rather sharp—hair profuse, and corresponding in colour with his eyes—limbs well proportioned—of strong muscular power—and a gait betraying self-confidence and independence.

Such is the outline of Mary's husband. There was about him a degree of mind—a certain education of thought and feeling, rarely to be met with in his tribe. Unlike many of the Indians on the frontiers of civilized districts, he never indulged in the use of ardent spirits—he seemed conscious of its tendency to degrade the man beneath the level of the brute, and appeared to shun contamination. The compressed expression of his mouth indicated resolution and firmness, and often have I endeavoured, in vain, to elicit from him a smile.

I have attempted at times to solve the mystery of this Indian's never-smiling face, and to form some conjecture as to the cause of the thoughtful and determined expression, which seemed to have no moments of relaxation upon his stern countenance.

Subsequent events have convinced me, that mighty and important thoughts were then working in the deep recesses of his untutored mind. I am now convinced he was ruminating upon the wrongs of his depressed and earth-trampled people—the serious injuries they had sustained, and the iniquities to which he saw himself and his tribe exposed, excited in his breast hatred and revenge; these constantly depressed his spirits—gave a colouring to his every thought, and cast a shadow of care over his intellectual brow.

The elder of this Indian family was Estalika, a girl of about fifteen years of age; her face beamed with animation—her features were not beautifully regular, but the *tout ensemble* of her countenance was such as the most fastidious in judgment of female beauty, could not but allow to be fascinating. She was the only one of Mary's children who had not that defect in vision similar to her mother.

Estalika had the clear olive-red complexion, the snow-white teeth, and the liquid-melting dark gazelle eyes of the beautiful daughters of the sunny clime—

" Where the virgins are soft as the roses they twine."

She was possessed of the vivacity of the playful fawn—which her name implies—with a large share of its timidity, combined however with a good degree of firmness; when rebuked, a crimson blush would suffuse her sweet face— but no tears, nor any other childish expressions of sorrow. Her young heart was like highly-polished steel—a breath could dim it for one moment, but the next restored its lustre.

An amiable family on the St. John's, won by

her gentleness of mind, received her into the house, and endeavoured to impart to her the blessings of civilized life; but her spirit drooped like a caged bird—she would often steal away, and wander alone for hours in her native forests, warbling some wild melody in the language of nature. Sometimes she would resort to the river, and launch a little canoe, and paddle along its picturesque banks—or into some retired creek, where she would hold communion with the natural beauties of the mysterious world around her; and, as she saw herself reflected in the dark watery mirror, she would dwell with innocent pride upon the beauty of her own form, or rather the gay costume of civilized life, to which her eye had not been hitherto accustomed.

On one occasion, being requested by the lady of the house to fetch some articles for her infant, which Estalika used to nurse, at a single bound she flew through the open window, and returned in the same manner; and when requested that she would in future give preference to the door, she replied "Cha!—this way quick—door too much far," and in a few moments, much to the amusement of the company, away she flew, like a bird, through the same aperture.

Nothing could tame this wood-nymph; in a few days her joyous shouts were heard resounding through the pine forest, in full exuberance of heart; she now roamed unrestrained through their well-known haunts, until she took possession of her light canoe, in which she paddled up the river many miles, to the wigwams of her tribe.

Indian Mary had many friends among the white inhabitants of Florida, and no sooner was she apprised that the Chiefs had held a council of war, than, in gratitude for the many kindnesses she had received from the "pale faces," she hastened to inform them of the danger which awaited them, unless they removed before Christmas.

This kind-hearted, artless Indian, fell a victim to her indiscreet benevolence, *indirectly*, through the very individuals she sought to rescue. The whites laughed at her surmises, and made a public jest of her admonitions. The consequence was fatal to poor Mary — her tribe obtained information of her apparent unfaithfulness, and she died the death of a traitress.

Estalika was subsequently obliged to endure hardships and privations to which her constitution was unequal, and which, aided by grief for the loss of her mother, threw her into a decline — she was taken, with other female Indians and children, by the whites, and confined in the fortress at St. Augustine; where the wild flower that had bloomed in loveliness but a few sunny days, was doomed to perish. She now sleeps with many others of her tribe, who breathed their last in those loathsome dungeons.

We have said that a secret sorrow seemed to brood over the mind of Yaha-Ematkla-Chupka; rugged and stern as seemed the outward man, he possessed all the kind feelings of a father—he loved his Estalika to devotion. There was a military officer, of some distinction, but a libertine in heart, who, struck with the beauty of this innocent child of nature, and considering it no difficult task to win her affections, took little pains to conceal his villainous designs; but Estalika, though an Indian not of the highest cast, had been trained with every virtuous feeling, and she indignantly bade him 'begone.'

It was something humiliating for this *mighty man* to be scorned by a *low-born savage*—and he determined to be revenged, and at the same time to prove his power over one he considered so much beneath him; but the GREAT SPIRIT watched over the girl, and before Major S——had time to approach her, she had fled with the speed of the wind to her father's protecting arms, and, amidst sighs and tears, related the story of her escape.

This circumstance alone would have been sufficient to incite him to revenge, but there were also his nation's many wrongs. The secret workings of his mind had at length approximated to maturity. Although he unquestionably sanctioned the decree of the Indian council against his wife, he looked forward with hope for the first act, of many since performed, in the bloody tragedy of the Seminole war. Nor was it long before an opportunity was afforded him to revenge the insult offered to his daughter, and to take up arms in defence of his country.

The war had no sooner commenced than he slew the foul tempter of his child, and heading one of the marauding parties sent out by

Oceola, he has been unremitting in his exertions to devastate the territory; and his revenge for his suffering people has no doubt been satiated; and probably the rigid muscles of his swarthy countenance have relaxed into more than one broad-grin of triumph, as he swung the tomahawk around the devoted heads of his " pale-faced" enemies.

There is an apology for the Indian the white man cannot plead—consanguineous attachment is as strong in one race as the other, and revenge for injuries committed against relatives comprise no inconsiderable portion of the civil and religious duty of the former; while, on the other hand, the religion of the SAVIOUR OF MANKIND inculcates forgiveness—discountenances revenge, and urges upon us, by the most important considerations, the cultivation of kindly feelings, even towards those who " despitefully use and persecute us."

An Indian is taught from childhood, that if one of his relatives should be killed, whether by accident or design, that the shade of the defunct must be appeased by the blood of the destroyer. Years may elapse, but time, the grand calmer of almost every passion, cannot render this quiescent.

Many instances are known of individuals who, having slain an Indian, have fled from the vicinity, and returned after an absence of many years; they lulled themselves into fatal security under the conviction of the circumstances being forgotten; but no sooner had intelligence of their arrival been communicated to the relatives of the deceased, than the homicides have been sacrificed.

The Seminoles are an intrepid race, "lofty in heart, in courage fierce, and in war delighting;" contending for the burial-place of their fathers, and their hunting-grounds—they are contending for their own homes and fire-sides—a patrimonial inheritance, transmitted from age to age, through a long line of ancestors; the blood of whom, in fierce struggles for the same soil, was poured out upon the altar of Liberty for its defence—and whose relics yet moulder beneath the mounds thrown up to their memory, to endear and consecrate the land.

The present generation are still struggling for their birth-rights, and will contest the innovations of their enemies to the last man. Death has no terrors for the Indian—who is taught to believe, that those who fall in battle, contending for the land given to them by the GREAT SPIRIT OF LIFE, ascend directly to HIM, who, at once introduces them to his own beautiful hunting-grounds—where are forests blooming in perpetual verdure and freshness — a sky that is never dimmed by a cloud—an air laden with fragrance—and where they pass an eternity in cool shades, beside running brooks; never to endure the toils of the chase, because the game is sleeping in every nook and dell.

And they believe, that here also they will mingle with the long, long succession of brave warriors, who have preceded them—that they will rejoice for ever with these spiritual existences, in perpetual youth and vigour; knowing neither sickness nor decay. Firmly believing this, as they do, and having every thing to gain by victory, is it not natural to suppose they will fight like gladiators, and if doomed to perish, exult in the last agonies of expiring nature?

If the whites are victorious, a grand and desperate tragedy is to be acted! The Seminoles have declared their determination to fight until the last solitary being of all the red men, who now people the wilderness of Florida, has perished!

Ought we to expect that the Indians, who

owned these lands by an undoubted and immemorial right of possession — who had ever ranged as freely upon them as the breezes which swept over their flowers, or waved the branches of the stupendous trees—should feel no indignation at the continued encroachments of white men?

The Americans seem to have forgotten, in their own injuries, and their sympathy for their ancestors, that the Indians are men of human feelings!—and that the ties which bound them to their native soil, were as strong as those which endeared the descendants of the conquerors of Troy to the land of Ulysses.

Though the radience of past glory lingered round the summits of the red man's uncultivated hills—though they never had a Parnassus consecrated to the Muses—nor a Parthenon lifting its costly and elegant front to the heavens—yet, here their fathers had lived—here had been the home of their youth—the theatre of their boyish pastimes and sports. The land was hallowed by a thousand tender and fondly cherished associations; and here, in the GREAT TEMPLE OF NATURE, amid the vast solitudes of their native forests was the place, where from the fulness of grateful and overflowing hearts, they had poured forth their fervent rejoicings to the GREAT SPIRIT.

But the work of extermination is still progressing — they are fast fading away; a few, comparatively, of the wretched tribes are yet remaining, in testimony *that they were;* their squalid, miserable condition, and appearance of degradation (particularly those upon the frontiers), tell of the light, knowledge, and immaculate blessings which civilization has dispensed to them. The waves of a rapidly increasing population are still booming on, and, ere long, they will have settled over them for ever!

Future generations will feel an interest in the achievements and history of the original inhabitants of America, of which we cannot now conceive. Legends of them, which shall have survived the wreck of time, will be sought after with avidity, to be gathered up and preserved as invaluable. Posterity will do justice to their characters, though it may not be done till after the last solitary being of all the numerous tribes, which once covered the face of this vast continent, has perished. Yet, justice will be done them; and the youth, the man of vigour, and the aged, of future generations, will weep and melt as they listen to a recital of the red man's wrongs.

I have already said, that Oceola preferred the wilder amusements of the woods to domestic life. During the early part of my retirement to my property at St. John's, where I had founded a town of that name, I undertook to open a road of communication to St. Augustine, upwards of forty miles; and, being anxious to complete my labor as speedily as possible, I deemed it necessary that I should be continually with the negroes, hired for the purpose of constructing bridges, felling trees, and cutting through dense swamps, &c. I took with me a small tent, for the use of myself and my little *protegée;* and, at night, with the overseer and negroes, we formed an encampment in the pine-forest—when, with blazing fires, surrounded by merry-grinning black faces, our time passed away pleasantly enough.

Early in the mornings my little friend would wake, and allow me no more quiet until I arose, which was generally at the first dawn of day; he would then make the woods re-echo with his joy—whooping and yelling, bounding round the pine trees, and exhibiting, in every possible way, the joyous feelings and exuberant spirits of laughter-loving childhood. He was very fond of accompanying me with my gun and dog, and would sometimes laugh heartily at the unsuccessfulness of my sport.

Nothing can ever efface from my memory one Sunday night, when the overseer had left us to visit his friends in St. Augustine. We were, with a dozen negroes, in a part of the forest that had not been visited by as many white people since the country was owned by the Spaniards. Throughout the universe, a wilder spot could not be selected than the "Three Runs;" over which we had to build bridges and form a causeway of six hundred paces.

These three black-looking streams meandered through a deep narrow valley, whose whole course formed a morass of thick jungle, shaded by the largest and most magnificent trees in the world. Here was, in stately grandeur, the gigantic live oak, with its thousand robes of moss — the splendid magnolia — cedar — wild orange—hickory; and here lurked in security, the shy and savage panther—the bear—and the wolf—with snakes of the most venomous description—and the hideous alligator.

Our encampment was upon the high ground on the south side of the 'hammock' I have just described, which sheltered us from the bleak north-wind. We had but three tents, two horses, two carts, and several dogs belonging to the negroes.—There were three very large fires made of the resinous pine logs, which threw up a glare of light, that gave to the dense woods in our rear a shade as dark as Erebus. About ten o'clock the full broad moon threw her silvery beams through the tall stately pines which sighed mournfully to the breeze.—Save this melancholy sound, with the dismal hooping of the owl—with, now and then the howling wolves at a distance — all was still, desolate, and dreary.

At this solemn moment, I reflected upon the condition of the slaves by whom I was surrounded.—'Tis true they were then happy—as they were the whole time while in my employ—I knew that this contentment was solely a relative feeling; a negro always comforts himself with having got rid of the past—he seldom reflects upon the future; if there be ever so small a chance of temporary happiness, he readily embraces it without embittering the moment by gloomy forebodings. They did not hear the crack of the 'Drivers'' whip, and they were happy. Under an impression that I might in some measure benefit them by wholesome admonition, and comfort them by prayer, I ordered them into the open space in the centre of the camp fires, and forming them into a circle, I placed the young Indian on his knees, and desired him to repeat *The Lord's Prayer.* No sooner had he raised his little plaintive voice to

Heaven, than the negroes followed his example with fervour and devotion. Here was a scene that might have softened the heart of the most obdurate sceptic— the sight of this young savage in his native wilds, offering up his orisons to Almighty God, accompanied by slaves even less informed than himself upon the attributes of prayer—with the solemn stillness of the wilderness, combined to make this the most impressive scene I had ever witnessed.

The prayer ended, I addressed them upon the peculiarity of their position in the human family; and endeavoured to ameliorate their condition by pouring a balm into the iron galls of slavery. I pointed out to them the necessity of obedience to their masters, and to depend upon their own worthiness for comfort and happiness. I assured them (and with truth) that their wants were fewer than many others of the human race—and, although not by the hand of kindness, they were supplied with all that was absolutely requisite for their subsistence—that it was to the interest of their proprietors to keep them in health, for their profits depended upon the negroes' physical strength. I advised them to rely upon a just God; and assured them that, by maintaining a virtuous and good life, one day they would find their reward.

A month passed in this way in the woods, at no little *risque* of an attack by Indians, who would have been glad to have availed themselves of our guns and horses.

I once took Oceola into St. Augustine, and showed him the Fort where his uncle and other Indian prisoners had been confined, and where many of them had perished from mephitic air. He was then not more than seven years of age; yet the sight of the dark frowning battlements, evidently struck a chill into his young heart, and he dreaded to meet any of the military — In fact, I could not reconcile him to the sight of a soldier. Being under some apprehension that he might be noticed by officers about the garrison, and perhaps claimed as a prisoner, I retreated to the woods early in the morning. As soon as he again breathed the free pure air of the Forest, the buoyancy of his spirit returned, and he again exhibited his usual manifestations of delight.

OTTER HUNT.

"Would ye preserve a num'rous finny race—
Let your fierce dogs the rav'nous otter chase."

GAY.

Riding with Oceola through the beautiful woods in the rear of my dwelling in St. John's, my dog drove a large otter across the road just before us—in an instant the boy was in pursuit through thick jungle, frequently, much obstructed by briers and other prickly bushes—but he wound his way with the celerity of a snake. He had not proceeded far before the animal backed himself against a tree, and showed fight—Now, a large otter is *an ugly customer* for a single dog; therefore my gallant 'Boxer,' deeming—

"Discretion the better part of valour"—

kept his enemy at bay until the arrival of the young huntsman; at the sight of whom, the otter made a fresh start—now and then resting himself against a tree, grinning defiance at his deadly foe; until, at last, Boxer drove him into an open field, when it became a running fight; which gave Oceola an opportunity of aiding his canine companion;—this he did by beating the otter with a stick until he was overpowered. In this encounter, there was considerable risk of his being severely bitten—the result of the action was in favor of my boy and the dog. He must have ran at least a mile through the bushes before the animal was killed: he then dragged home the body, weighing 25-lbs., a mile and a half. Returning, he gave a preference to the open fields, which augmented the distance—he could only advance a few paces with his load, and then rest: and in this way did he persevere, until he reached home—almost exhausted by fatigue, but highly proud of his achievement.

This little incident showed a perseverance, courage, and determination of an extraordinary character, in one so young—few would have withstood the scratches, the toil, and hunger he endured for a whole day—for the sole reward of commendation, or the gratification of the sport.

The conduct of Oceola so far gained upon my regard, that I fully determined to adopt and cherish him as my own child. His welfare seemed now wholly to depend upon my exertions. From the jealousy and undisguised hostility of my white neighbours, I perceived that his safety was endangered, independent of the risk of his being claimed by the authorities and "sent west."—Apprehensive of this, we sought for him a secure retreat in the dense woods at the back of my dwelling—to which we instructed him to retire on the least warning of danger. The approach of a steam-boat on the river, or the landing of strangers, roused our anxiety, when we would despatch him to his place of concealment, with instructions to remain until he heard our preconcerted signal.

His happiness and future success in life seemed now to depend wholly upon himself—here he was an outcast from civilized society, excepting that of my own family—his parents or friends either dead or transported upwards of a thousand miles into a strange land—whither he would probably be sent, if taken from my protection, without even the power to express his wants—having forgotten his vernacular tongue; and where hundreds of his tribe had already perished, through the effects of change from a low to a higher latitude.

Under all these disadvantages, without regard to personal interest, I resolved to rescue this poor child from a prospect of misery and destitution. Among the whites in Florida it was evident that my protection would not long prove his safeguard; and most ardently did I long for the security and freedom of 'my native land.'

My determination to embark for England with my young charge, was soon fixed, and almost as soon executed; and I joyfully left this blood-stained country on Thursday, the 28th of May, 1840, and arrived in Savannah on the following Saturday.

Young Oceola expressed much delight on beholding the cotton ships—hitherto he had seen no larger vessels than coasting schooners on the St. John's river. As speedily as possible I placed him on board a ship bound for Liverpool. Here, he did not seem secure from his enemies; the Captain assured me that he ran considerable risk in receiving him on board, as he was known to be a young Indian highly connected in the Seminole nation; but an Almighty Providence, who watches the destinies of the fatherless, has hitherto protected the *Orphan Boy*.

On the 4th of June we left the shores of America, and reached Liverpool in safety on Thursday night, the 2nd of July, and landed on the following morning.

During our passage, Oceola became the darling of the sailors, who were delighted with his exploits and agility in climbing the rigging to the tops of the masts, and on landing they parted with him with reluctance.

Even in Liverpool, the Captain and my fellow-passengers expressed an apprehension that the American Consul would claim the young Prince, and send him back a prisoner to the United States. I laughed at the absurdity of such a suggestion—relying with implicit confidence on the hospitable character of my countrymen for protection of my boy. He was now (it may truly be said,) in the land of freedom; where I rejoiced to find myself once more—after an absence of twenty years.

Oceola here met with the kindest attention from the amiable family of Mr. Callan—to whom I shall ever feel grateful for their hospitality, both towards my *protegée* and myself, during the few days we remained in Liverpool. Strangely enough, a young Son of the American Consul was at the time on a visit to Mr. Callan, and became the constant companion and playmate of Oceola; and, had the Consul himself been in town, I feel well assured my young friend would have been by him also kindly received.

Since he has been in London, he has met with the most flattering marks of attention from persons of rank and respectability. His chief amusement, during his leisure moments from school, has been to visit Mr. Catlin's exhibition at the Egyptian Hall; and sometimes I have yielded to the entreaties of himself and his friends, in permitting him to appear in his native costume before the public. My principal motive in so doing has been, that he might retain in his memory the scenes of his childhood, and learn more of the history of his people. I cannot forbear once more reverting to Mr. Catlin and his collection of Indian costumes and curiosities.

This enterprising artist has undoubtedly undergone more labour and privation in obtaining a knowledge of this primitive race of men, than any other North American Traveller. Eight of his best years have been devoted to the pursuit of this branch of science; and he has succeeded in amassing an immense collection of dresses, spears, bows and arrows, pipes, scalps—a large wigwam, or Indian tent—with many hundreds of other curious articles; besides which, he has taken portraits of upwards of three hundred of the most distinguished Chiefs — and painted many beautiful views of American scenery, in parts hitherto unknown to civilized man.

When we reflect that the tribes of Indians are daily dwindling from the face of the earth, and had not Mr. Catlin rescued so much of their works from oblivion, but few records would now be in existence to hand down to future ages a pictorial history, with such ample testimony of the manners, customs, nay, even the existence of this noble class of human beings.

How much, then, does Mr. Catlin merit the gratitude of all civilized nations!

I appeal, as an Englishman, to the people of this country, who have always been liberal patrons of the Fine Arts — who have always evinced an enthusiastic sympathy for the

Aborigines of all nations — if these splendid productions should be permitted to leave England to ornament the Museum of some Foreign nation.

They are the manufactory of a people who know no arts or sciences, but such as those pointed out by Nature herself—to guard them from the inclemencies of the weather—to provide them with food, and to repel their enemies; manifesting, at the same time, talents of no ordinary character: proving, beyond doubt, their capabilities to attain the highest order of intellectual refinement.

Ought not then the scientific people of England endeavour to procure these interesting collections as curiosities worthy to rank with those from Pompeii, Palmyra, or with the rarest specimens of Ancient or Modern Artists? What other evidence will posterity have of the bare existence of the Tribes of Western India!

Already whole tribes have been swept away, and scarcely any other relic left of them—save what is now in the keeping of this champion for Indian character and Indian rights. Where are now the Mandans — the Mohicans — the Yemasseés—and many other once formidable and numerous tribes?—They are gone from the earth, and will, ere long, be effaced from the memory of man!

Little more than two centuries have elapsed, since the first permanent settlements were made upon the American wilderness: yet this short period has sufficed to change the character of a continent—to produce the entire destruction of what were once powerful tribes—and, almost, the extermination of a RACE!!

The vices of the whites have penetrated even among some of the tribes of the "far distant West." The subtle poison of the Harpies—called Indian Traders—has begun to sap the foundations of their original nobleness of character; and at no distant day — of the thousands and tens of thousands who once dwelt within the limits of the United States, only here and there will a wanderer remain.

As from the short period of two hundred years, we turn back and attempt to gather the customs and traditions of the tribes which dwelt within the limits of New England, anterior to the arrival of the whites—we find only scattered fragments, detached and confused—no relic is left of their history or habits; and scarcely anything is known of them, unless—that *they are gathered to their fathers!*

The tribes on the outskirts of civilization are fast disappearing; and the period will soon have arrived, when their joys and sorrows will be at an end—when they will be beyond the reach of duplicity and extortion: and, surely, justice demands that some record of their rude virtues, and unhappy fate, should be traced on the pages of history, or be carefully preserved in the archives of some enlightened nation.

FINIS

APPENDIX.

We have already said that the Chief, Oceola, was interred in consecrated ground near Charleston; but will it be credited, that with all the display of sympathy for a fallen hero, whose fame has been re-echoed in every village throughout the United States—whose name has been conspicuous in all the newspapers of the north, with which was coupled that of his betrayer, General Jessup, whom they loaded with curses dire and deep—that, in defiance of all this excitement in favor of Oceola, he was *buried headless!* Dr. Weedon, with the knowledge and consent of the officers who had charge of the remains of this brave and distinguished man, so far violated the sacred remains of the dead; which the foul mercenary had conveyed to New York, there to be exhibited in Peale's museum, with other heads of New Zealand chiefs. These disgusting peparations, in themselves, were sufficiently disgraceful, without the addition of one, which in life had held millions in defiance.

This outrage upon the feelings and decency of the inhabitants of New York, soon roused their resentment. When it was announced to the public that THE HEAD OF OCEOLA was to be seen at Peale's Museum, in Broadway, a mob collected, and threatened to raze the building to the ground, if this disgusting object were not forthwith removed. It was accordingly taken away by *the Doctor*, who conveyed it to St. Augustine, in Florida, where finding he could not *make a raise* upon it, placed it in spirits on the counter of his "drug store," for the gratuitous gratification of poor Oceola's enemies.

"To what base uses we may return, Horatio."

Extract of a Letter from CAPT. BELL, *to* H. S. DEXTER, ESQ. *Dated " Volusia, September* 18*th*, 1821.

"'As I am under an engagement to accompany Econchatti-Mico, the King, and all the chiefs and head men to St. Augustine, I shall defer, until my arrival at that place, the substance of their deliberation and "talk," all of which I have noted, as I was certain it would be gratifying to you.

*　　*　　*　　*

"I have not the pleasure of being acquainted with our new Governor, and will thank you to apprise him of the intended visit of the Indians, headed by their Chief or King, Econchatti-Mico."

*　　*　　*　　*

H. S. DEXTER *to* CAPT. BELL.—*St. Augustine, July* 30, 1822.

* * * *

" Econchatti, the Seminole King, assisted by his principal Counsellors, met in Council on the 24th of May, at our settlement at Allachua, and delivered to us a ' talk,' relating to their present situation and future prospects, &c. &c."

" On Wednesday, the 20th inst., while a lieutenant and two men were passing between Micanopy and a place called ' Black Point,' they were surprised, and fired on by a party of Indians; the lieutenant and one man wounded, and one killed. Same evening, Lieut. Sanderson, in command of Micanopy, while on a scout with eighteen or twenty men, discovered a fire in the woods, and on going to see from whence it proceeded, was surrounded by about fifty Indians; Lieut. S. and *nine* men, three BLOOD-HOUNDS and their keeper, killed upon the spot, and four men missing. On Friday, news reached Newnansville, that three men were killed between Posts No. 11 and 12. On Thursday, a scout discovered the trail of about 100 Indians in the 'Wolf Hammock,' six miles south of Newnansville."—*East Florida Advocate.*

" The BLOOD-HOUNDS sent for by Governor Call have arrived at Tallahassee, accompanied by twenty Leashmen, from the Island of Cuba; we hope soon to hear they are on the scent of the enemy."—*St. Augustine News.*

The first trial made by these dogs, was upon the trail of one Indian, whom they literally tore in pieces; several women and children were subsequently taken, dreadfully lacerated by the teeth of these ferocious animals.

In a speech delivered in the House of Representatives of the United States, by Mr. White of Florida, we can readily account for the objections of the Seminole Indians to emigrate to lands on the western side of the Mississippi. When such few of this tribe had agreed to the treaty of their removal, they had not then learned how their neighbours, the Cherokees, had been decoyed from the homes of their fathers. We find in the speech alluded to, as follows:—

"Some five years ago, a treaty had been negotiated with the Cherokees, by which lands were ceded to them on the west of the Mississippi, a territory, as was presumed, beyond the reach of settlement, as it had been beyond the reach of surveys. When the Indians, under this treaty, went to take possession of these lands, they found other settlers upon them, and at the very last Congress an act had passed, giving pre-emption rights to the individuals who had been found there.

Thus the poor deluded Indians, many hundred miles from their native homes, without the means of returning, were compelled to shift for themselves in the best way they could. Poverty and change of climate soon induced sickness, of which a greater portion perished.

THE TREATY OF MOULTRIE CREEK.

1824.

JAMES MONROE, PRESIDENT OF THE UNITED STATES OF AMERICA.

To all and singular to whom these Presents shall come, greeting.—

WHEREAS a Treaty between the Unites States of America and the Florida Tribes of Indians, was made and concluded on the 18th day of September, 1823, at Camp, on Moultrie Creek, in the Territory of Florida, by Commissioners on the part of the United States, and certain Chiefs and Warriors of the said Tribes, on the part and in behalf of the said Tribes, which Treaty is in the following words, to wit:—

Article 1.—The undersigned Chiefs and Warriors, for themselves and their Tribes, have appealed to the humanity, and thrown themselves on, and have promised to continue under the protection of the United States, and of no other

Nation, Power, or Sovereign; and in consideration of the promises and stipulations hereinafter made, do cede and relinquish all claim or title which they may have to the whole Territory of Florida, with the exception of such district of Country, as shall be herein allotted them.

Article 2.—The Florida Tribes of Indians will hereafter be concentrated and confined to the following Metes and Boundaries; commencing five miles North of Okehumke, running in a direct line to a point, five miles West of Setarky's settlement, on the waters of the Amazura or Ouithlacoochee River, leaving said settlement two miles South of the line, from thence in a direct line to the South end of the Big Hammock, to include Chikkuchatti; continuing on in the same direction for five miles beyond the said Hammock; provided said point does not approach nearer than fifteen miles the sea Coast of the Gulph of Mexico; if it does, the said line will terminate at that distance from the sea Coast; thence South twelve miles, thence in a South 30° East direction. until the same shall strike within five miles of the main branch of the Charlotte River, thence in a due East direction to within twenty miles of the Atlantic Coast; thence North fifteen, West for fifty miles— and from this last to the beginning point.

Article 3.—The United States will take the Florida Indians under their care and patronage, and will afford them protection against all persons whatsoever, provided they conform to the Laws of the United States, and refrain from making War, or giving any insult to any Foreign Nation, without having first obtained the permission and consent of the United States. And, in consideration of the appeal and cession made in the 1st Article of this Treaty, by the aforesaid Chiefs and Warriors, the United States promise to distribute among the Tribes, as soon as concentrated under the direction of their Agent, implements of husbandry, and stocks of cattle and hogs, to the amount of six thousand dollars, and an annual sum of five thousand dollars a year, for twenty successive years—to be distributed as the President of the United States shall direct, through the Secretary-of-War, or his Superintendents and Agents of Indian affairs.

Article 4.—The United States promise to guarantee to the said Tribes, the peaceable possession of the district of Country assigned them, reserving the right of opening through it such roads, as may from time to time be deemed necessary, and to restrain and prevent all white persons from hunting, settling, or otherwise intruding upon it. But any Citizen of the United States, being lawfully authorized for that purpose, shall be permitted to pass and repass through said District, and to navigate the waters thereof, without any hindrance, toll, or exaction from said Tribes.

Article 5.—For the purpose of facilitating the removal of said Tribes to the District of country allotted them, and as a compensation for the losses sustained, or the inconveniences to which they may be exposed by said removal, the

United States will furnish them with rations of corn, meat, and salt, for twelve months, commencing on the 1st day of February next.

And they further agree to compensate those individuals who have been compelled to abandon improvements on lands not embraced within the limits allotted, to the amount of four thousand five hundred dollars, to be distributed among the sufferers, in a ratio to each, proportional to the value of the improvements abandoned. The United States further agree, to furnish a sum not exceeding two thousand dollars, to be expended by their Agent, to facilitate the transportation of the different Tribes to the point of concentration designated.

Article 6.—An Agent, Sub-Agent, and Interpreter, shall be appointed to reside within the Indian Boundary aforesaid, to watch over the interest of said Tribes. And the United States further stipulate, as an evidence of their humane policy towards said tribes who have appealed to their liberality, to allow for the establishment of a School at the Agency, one thousand dollars per year, for twenty successive years; and one thousand dollars per year, for the same period, for the support of a Gun and Black-Smith, with the expenses incidental to his shop.

Article 7.—The Chiefs and Warriors aforesaid, for themselves and Tribes, stipulate to be active and vigilant in the preventing the retreating to, or passing through of the district of country assigned them, of any absconding slave, or fugitives from justice, and further agree to use all necessary exertions to apprehend and deliver the same to the agent, who shall receive orders to compensate them agreeably to the trouble and expences incurred.

Article 8.—A Commissioner or Commissioners, with a Surveyor, shall be appointed by the President of the United States, to run and mark (blazing fore and aft the trees) the line, as defined in the second article of this Treaty; who shall be attended by a Chief or Warrior, to be designated by a Council of their own Tribe, and who shall receive, while so employed, a daily compensation of three dollars.

Article 9.—The undersigned Chiefs and Warriors, for themselves and Tribes, having objected to their concentration within the limits described in the second article of this Treaty, under the impression that the said limits did not contain a sufficient quantity of good land for them to subsist on, and for other reasons—It is therefore expressly understood between the United States and the aforesaid Chiefs and Warriors, that should the country embraced in said limits, upon examination by the Indian Agent, and the Commissioner or Commissioners, to be appointed under the eighth article of this Treaty, be by them considered insufficient for the support of the said Indians, then the north line, as defined in the second article of this Treaty, shall be removed so far north as to embrace a sufficient quantity of good, tillable land.

Article 10.—The undersigned Chiefs and Warriors, for themselves and Tribes, have expressed to the Commissioners their unlimited confidence in their agent, Colonel Gad Humphreys, and their interpreter, Stephen Richards; and as evidence of their gratitude for their services and humane treatment, and brotherly attentions to their wants, request that one mile square, embracing the improvements of Ewe-Mathla, at Tallahassee, (said improvements to be considered as the centre) be conveyed in fee-simple, as a present to Colonel Gad Hamphreys. And they further request, that one mile square at the Ocheesee Bluffs, embracing Stephen Richards' field on said Bluffs, be conveyed in fee-simple, as a present to Stephen Richards. The Commissioners accord in sentiment with the undersigned Chiefs and Warriors, and recommend a compliance with their wishes to the President and Senate of the United States; but the disapproval, on the part of the said authorities, of this article, shall in nowise affect the other articles and stipulations concluded on in this Treaty.

In testimony whereof, the Commissioners, William P. Duval, James Gadsden, and Bernard Segui, and the undersigned Chiefs and Warriors, have hereunto subscribed their names and affixed their seals.

Done at the camp on Moultrie Creek, in the Territory of Florida, this 18th day of September, 1823, and of the Independence of the United States, the forty-eighth.

William P. Duval	Econchatti-Mico
James Gadsden	Nea Mathkla, × his mark
Bernard Segui	Tokose Mathkla

Ninnee Homata Tustenuggee Lathlon Mathla
Miconopy   Senufky
Necosee Apola   Alak Hajo
John Blunt   Faheluste Hajo
Ottemata   Octapamico
Tuskeneka   Tustenec Hajo
Tuske Hajo   Okoske Amathla
Emoteley   Ochanee Tustenuggee
Mulato King   Philip
Chocolohano   Charley Amathkla
Ematlochee   John Hassorey
Wekse Holata   Rathead
Amathla Ho   Holata Amathkla
Holataficico   Foschatti-Mico
Cheficico Hajo

Signed, sealed, and delivered in presence of George Murray, Secretary to the Commission.

   Gad Humphreys, Indian Agent.
   Stephen Richards, Interpreter.
   Isaac N. Cox.
   I. Irving, Captain 4th Artillery.
   Harvey Brown, Lieutenant 4th Artillery.
   C. D'Espinville, Lieutenant 4th Artillery.
   John B. Scott, Lieutenant 4th Artillery.
   William Travers.
   Horatio S. Dexter.

Let us examine a little into the merits of this much talked of Treaty, in the United States, for which the Indians are held up to the world as "treacherous villains," in not having conformed to the articles therein mentioned;—as having "violated the Treaty."

Whilst in Florida, I had frequent conferences with Mr. Travers upon the subject of "Treaties," the results of which I shall endeavour to bring to bear upon that of "Moultrie Creek," commencing with

Article 1.—Which specifies that "*the undersigned Chiefs and Warriors, for themselves and their Tribes,* HAVE APPEALED TO THE HUMANITY, *and thrown themselves on, and have promised to continue under the protection of the United States, &c.* The Chiefs and Warriors of the Seminole Tribes, would spurn the idea of appealing to the humanity of the United States, under any circumstances; which has been sufficiently proved during the last five years; during which time, they have shed their blood, drop by drop, and themselves, with their wives and children, have fallen, one by one, into the hands of their enemies—the United States;—still they have never appealed to *their humanity*, and happy had it been for them had they remained under the Government of Spain, when their rights were respected—they were then free and independent.

The Spanish Floridians knew the value of these people—the markets of St. Augustine, Pensacola, and other towns in the colony, were well supplied with venison, and all the game the country produced, besides cattle and skins to a considerable amount; and whenever the Chiefs condescended to visit the governor, they were received with kindness and dismissed with presents; their wrongs from white men were speedily redressed, and when the Spaniards required their aid in war, they proved valuable allies.

Article 2.—The line of boundary run by the United States was never agreed to on the parts of the Chiefs, generally; two or three alone were bribed to consent, with whiskey, and presents of rifles and ammunition.

Article 3.—The Seminolee Indians never did, or ever would be, made to conform to the laws of the United States; upon all occasions, they exercised their own ceremonies, and enforced their own laws upon each other; and their white neighbours knew that the death of one of the tribe, was sure to be succeeded by a reprisal—without waiting for the laws of the United States. And as to the bombast of implements of husbandry, stocks of cattle, to the amount of six thousand dollars *a year*, the *annual* sum of five thousand dollars, and the other stipulations, in behalf of the Indians —for further particulars enquire of Col. Gad Humphreys, and Major Phagan, the Indian agents.

I make no doubt, the Government paid *part* of this money into the hands of the aforesaid agents, who doled it out to the poor Indians, at the rate of two *choks* (10$d.$ sterling), per glass of whiskey, ditto for gunpowder—both combustibles were measured in the same vessel, and all other supplies were provided in the same ratio.

Articles 4 and 5.—All gammon.

Article 6.—*An agent to watch over the interest of the Indians*—like a hackney-coachman over the interest of his employer; so much for master, so much for me—so much for me, so much for master.

Article 7.—If the Seminolee Indians had occupied themselves in arresting white fugitives from justice, they would have had no time to hunt.

Article 8.—A few poor Red-skins, were made to carry the surveyor's chain—for which they got flogged, if not sufficiently active.

Article 9.—A mere humbug on the parts of the Commissioners, to give some appearance of character and justice to THE *TREATY!*

Article 10.—The perfection of knavery by the agent and interpreter—of so glaring a character that the Government would not stand it.

Now, this precious specimen of American bamboozle, with thirty-two Indian signatures—William Travers informed me was actually signed by only *six out of the whole*, and they were made drunk for that purpose; the remaining names were filled up by the Commissioners themselves.

The next Treaty, said to have been made at Payne's Landing, in May, 1832, is of a still more vile character than the last. That was for taking the whole territory from the Indians, and to send them away to the Arkansaw country. The manner in which that pretended agreement has been resisted, has already been explained. Like the one of 1823, it has been published in America, with the signatures of the principal Chiefs and Warriors—most of whom *never even saw it!*

CAST OF NIKKANOCHEE's HEAD.

A very correct cast of this child's head has been taken by Mr. Donovan, *Principal of the London Phrenological Institution,* King William Street, Strand.

The science, of which Mr. Donovan is a zealous teacher, and an able expounder, practically as well as theoretically, holds—" that as the moral and intellectual faculties are exercised, the development of the organs of those faculties will be assisted, and the shape of the upper and frontal regions made to approach nearer to the most perfect type of the human head.

" By a judicious mode of education, the animal propensities will be kept in abeyance, and not called into action (as they assuredly would have been) in this case, had the child remained in his native wilds. There, combativeness, secretiveness, and destructiveness, would have been continually called into operation ; nay, they would have been looked on as the highest intellectual virtues.

"Thus, then, education steps in to reverse this decree— the animal propensities are not encouraged—the moral sentiments and intellectual faculties are judiciously exercised; and, by these means, the *contour* of the head approaches more and more to that of man, in his most civilized state."

Mr. Donovan has made notes on this cast, and has kindly suggested some important points relating to education, &c. Previous to the moment I had the gratification of being made acquainted with this learned and benevolent gentleman, I acknowledge myself to have been a sceptic in the science of Phrenology; but, after having heard the subject so ably and clearly expounded by him, with such striking manifestations of the truth, as regards the effect of the education of thought on the conformation of the human skull, I can no longer withhold my expression of a thorough belief in the system of Phrenology, and do most strenuously recommend those who may wish to perfect themselves in this interesting and highly useful branch of polite learning, to attend to his lectures and discourses.

Since writing the above, Mr. Donovan has been kind enough to promise that casts of Prince Econchatti's head will be taken from time to time.—It will be interesting to observe the effect of education on the conformations of the brain, and the consequent changes in the shape of the head.

A splendid painting, similar to the frontispiece, has been made of the Young Prince, by Mr. WILKIN—which is now in the Exhibition at the Royal Academy, Trafalgar Square.

EXTRACTS FROM NEWSPAPERS.

Several other combinations were formed at different times by distinguished Indian Chiefs and patriots, to rescue their country from the hands of those whom they regarded as usurpers and intruders. They saw their once unbounded possessions gradually receding from them, their numerous tribes dwindling away, the graves of their fathers overturned by the ploughshare, and their hunting-ground converted into fields of grain, and occupied by men whom they had every reason to look upon as the enemies of their race. Their native courage, and a deep sense of the injury and wrongs under which they suffered, roused them to action, and their vengeance was sometimes terrible; but their vengeance was unavailing. They have gradually retired before the wave of the white population, yielded up their valuable lands, either by compulsion or persuasion, and buried themselves, from time to time, among the primeval forests and extensive prairies of their country, to be free and uncontaminated by the vices of civilization. But even there they found no security.

The arm of the pale-face, and his arts and liquid fire reached them. " As the tide of our population rolled on," says an eloquent Senator,* "we have added purchase to purchase; the confiding Indian listened to our professions of friendship. We called him brother, and he believed us. Millions after millions he has yielded to our importunity, until we have acquired more than can be cultivated in centuries, and yet we crave more. We have crowded the tribes upon a few miserable acres on our southern frontier: it is all that is left to them of their once boundless forests, and still, like the horse leech, our insatiable cupidity cries, give—give." This is a true picture of the treatment the aboriginal proprietors of the soil of America have received from their white brethren, since their arrival in this country. To complete the measure of injustice, the government has ordered the removal of all the Indian tribes still remaining beyond the Mississippi, where they are promised lands in lieu of those they have abandoned. Almost all these tribes have seen that it would be madness to resist the mandate of the government, and have retired to the west of the Mississippi. Some noble spirits, however, still hold out, and among these is the distinguished Seminole chief, Oceola. The Seminoles comprehend the remains of many tribes that formerly occupied the territory of Florida, and they are now reduced to a bare handful. The love of their native land

* Mr. Frelinghuysen, of New Jersey.

burns strongly in their bosoms, and Oceola has gallantly and nobly contended, with his small band, for the country and graves of his fathers. He has withstood the whole military force of the United States for nearly two years, and though captured, is still unconquered. The manner in which he has been taken is dishonorable to our arms, and disgraceful to the nation. He trusts to the honor of the whites, and, with that confidence, throws himself within their power, to negociate for the liberty of one of his countrymen—and what is the consequence? Finding that they cannot conquer him in fair and manly fight, they resort to a breach of faith, and take him prisoner by a superior force, while he is trusting to their honor. A gallant enemy would have said to him—"We have you now in our power, but you have confided in our faith, and we scorn to avail ourselves of our superiority; retire, and we will meet you in the battle field, and subdue you, if we can. The nation itself, if it possessed the least spirit of gallantry, should feel the deepest mortification at such an act, and at once grant this noble and patriotic Chieftain his liberty, and the right of remaining, with his whole tribe, and their descendants, for ever, in the country for which they have so bravely and manfully contended. But injustice is everywhere. No nation, whatever be the form of its government, or the character of its people, is, or ever has been exempt from it. When men feel power they are apt to forget right—the strong will trample upon the weak, and justice will always be more an abstraction than a reality. Cupidity and injustice will at last triumph, in spite of the efforts of philanthropy and benevolence, and the feeble remnants of a noble but untutored race, will soon be blotted for ever from the face of the world." *Washington Paper.*

CAPTURE OF KING PHILIP'S SON IN FLORIDA.—General Hernandez, of the Florida Militia, succeeded in capturing near Matanzas, Coacoochee (or Wild Cat), King Philip's Son. The *St. Augustine Herald* of the 28th ult, gives this picturesque account of him:—

" Coacoochee was mounted on a spirited horse, and attired in his native costume—he rode into town with a great deal of savage grace and majesty. His head-dress was a plume of white crane feathers and a silver band. He is now confined in the Fort, with his Father."

He subsequently made his escape with fifty of his Warriors, since which he has not been re-captured. He afterwards rode through the streets of St. Augustine in the evening, in full costume, accompanied by *five* of his Warriors.

The inhabitants of the Garrison and Fort, were so much astounded that they remained passive until he was fairly into the Pine Forests.—[AUTHOR.]

SURROUNDING THE ENEMY.—" In the *destruction of Indians* the other day, during a scout by Capt. Holmes, 7th Infantry, an instance of *coolness* and *bravery* occurred, exhibiting the *material of our own service*, and the indomitable courage of the Indian. Capt. Holmes had secreted a portion of his company in such a place as it was probable the enemy might pass, and proceeded onward with the rest of his command, in order *to hunt them up*. The ambushed party had not lain long in their hiding-place, when a *few* Indians were seen approaching, unconscious of their near proximity to the white man.—On nearing more closely, the anxiety of a *recruit* being more intense, was with difficulty restrained from breaking up the enemy, and probably defeating the great object in view. At this moment, a deer sprang from its covert, and passing within a few feet of his gun the temptation was too great, and the recruit fired.— Alarmed by the report, the enemy ran, and the *Sergeant*, with his command, mounted their horses and gave pursuit. The Serjeant soon overtook a large and very athletic Indian, and dismounting, *deliberately levelled his gun within a few feet of his breast, and pulled the trigger.* The gun missed fire; and the red-skin now levelled his rifle, and lo, the flint refused its duty! Dashing his musket to the earth, the Sergeant sprang to grapple his enemy, but was felled by the clubbed end of his rifle. Rising, he used the breach of his gun with good effect, but was repeatedly felled by the greater strength of his foe. Victory hanging now in a doubtful posture, he managed *while his head was receiving a succession of tremendous blows, to 'fix his bayonet,' and made a charge upon the herculean Seminole.* Doubt was at an end; the warrior took to his heels, and sought a tree. There dodging a direct thrust of the instrument, he managed to hold the anger of the Sergeant at bay, until *the balance of the command came up;* who, disposed to see 'a fair fight,' formed a circle around the combatants. All hope was now cut off; and *with a desperate valour he fought:* the Sergeant thrusting his bayonet through him, and laying him dead at his feet." –*St. Augustine News.*

INDIAN NEWS.—Our excellent correspondents at Black Creek have put us in possession of intelligence from Fort King to the 8th inst. which we give as follows:—

"On last Sunday week, Col. Riley ran down an Indian in the Pine Woods, near the Withlacoochee. A day or two afterwards, he surprised an Indian camp, consisting of two warriors, two squaws, and four children; they killed the two warriors and one squaw, and took the rest prisoners.— On Tuesday night last, one of the Indians made his escape, owing to the sentinel going to sleep. One of the guard saw him running, and fired at him, which alarmed the whole camp; the other sentinels also fired. Capt. Mason was shot dead, either by the Indians, or accidentally by his own men—it is supposed that the latter was the case. He was seen running after the Indian, and it is impossible to say who killed him."—*Florida Paper.*

The *Morning Herald* states that in the West of Ohio, flour is selling at two-and-a-half dollars per barrel, and that in 1836-7 it was fourteen dollars per barrel in New York.—The Indian war in Florida continues, and it seems to be one of extermination. The civilized whites have resorted to the barbarous practice of hunting down those whom they call savages, with *blood-hounds*, which have been imported from Cuba for the purpose. The following cool announcements appear in the *New York Morning Herald*:—"The *blood-hounds*, lately received from Cuba, have been subjected to many experiments, the results of which have been very satisfactory. They follow a trail twenty-four hours old with rapidity and accuracy. Some of them are to be employed by the troops now scouring the country, between the mouths of the Wacassassa and Suwannee Rivers, Micanopy, &c."

THE BLOOD-HOUNDS IN FULL CRY. "Major Bailey, with a party of dragoons, and six *blood-hounds*, scented out forty Indians recently in Florida, and killed six of them. Only one dog was killed."

If the truth could be known, we should probably find that the atrocities occasionally blazoned in the papers, for the purpose of inflaming the public mind, were nothing more, if they really occurred, than measures of retaliation for the perfidy and cruelty of the whites. Some of the States have remonstrated against the employment of blood-hounds, as a barbarous practice, and some memorials have been presented to Congress.—They were referred to the Committee on Military Affairs, which subsequently requested to be discharged from the consideration of the subject. The information received from the Secretary-at-War stated, that bloodhounds had certainly been employed for the purpose of hunting the Indians, but he did not "feel authorized to instruct the authorities of Florida not to employ them, for the reason that they might be used to advantage."

The news from Florida, in relation to the fugitive Indians in the vicinity of the Choctawhatchee Bay, is by no means satisfactory. A letter to the Editor of the *Pensacola Gazette*, dated at La Grange, on the 21st ult. gives an account of a fight near Black Creek, between *thirty-three* whites and a party of Indians—in which five of the latter were killed, and a child taken prisoner. Black Creek is about sixteen miles from La Grange. Another murder was committed at the Cow-ford, by the Indians, on the person of a Mr. Lawrence. On the 23rd, another fight took place at the Alaqua Creek, about five miles from La Grange—in which twelve Indians were killed, and ten made prisoners. The *Pensacola Gazette* adds the following paragraph :—" It is reported that the Indians killed were all, or nearly all, *prisoners;* that there was but one man among the slain— *the rest were women and children !*"

EXTRACT FROM COL. BAILY'S REPORT.—We encamped together that night, which was the 14th. I discovered considerable signs of Indians in the hammock, and had determined on going in again the next day on foot. On the 15th, in the morning, we went about two miles—fell in with Adjutant Norton, and his command of footmen, from whom I learned, that on the previous morning he had, with the *blood-hounds, which were very useful, trailed an Indian* into the hammock. On arriving in the hammock, found the sign very fresh, *and turned the dogs loose.* They went about 150 yards—came up and caught *one* of the Indians, and the principal *catch-dog* was killed. Immediately the men pursued after the other dogs, which were after the Indians, for six or eight miles, but could not come up, in consequence of the thickness of the swamp, &c.; but, judging from the *blood* on the trail, *one of the Indians must have been badly wounded.* Near the place where the dog was killed, he came upon an encampment from which the *families* had just escaped. On learning this the horsemen were all dismounted—a horse guard was arranged, and the balance of the men were formed into four detachments. I then sent two detachments to my left, and one to my right, and entered the hammock abreast. I had not gone more than a mile into the hammock, when we came suddenly upon a warrior, *who was brought down* by Capt. Hall, and charging onward, we came upon a large encampment, from which the approach of Adjutant Norton had evidently driven the *families* the previous morning, and if any warriors were hanging around, they made off without showing themselves.

The different detachments passed the day in endeavouring to follow the trails; but the nature of the grounds being low and swampy, intersected in all directions by ponds communicating with each other by 'runs' of water, through which the Indians travelled, rendered our labour unavailing.

These two encampments were about two miles south of the Jackson trail, and between the foot-log on the Econfonee and Thomas's Old Mills on the Finholloway. They had, I should judge, about twenty acres planted in pumpkins and squashes, but no corn that I could find. Crossing the Finholloway, we proceeded to the Esteenhatchee, scouting the country on both sides the road from Fort Andrews to Fort Frank-Brook, without discovering recent signs of Indians, which may perhaps be attributed to the scarcity of water in that section.

To the east of Esteenhatchee, near the Coast, I scouted five days with equally poor success.

On Thursday, the 28th of May, sending part of my command westward, I proceeded with the remainder to the 'pumpkin hammock,' in direct line, about six miles east of the rocky ford on the Esteenhatchee, where we, on Friday, the 29th, destroyed several fields of corn and pumpkins, &c. —returned to our horses at night, and on the next morning, Captains Hall and Townsend returned to the fields with fourteen men, to waylay. They started in the hammock at daylight, and at the usual time of leaving camp, I moved off with the horses, say about one and a half miles from the hammock, so as to deceive the Indians if they had discovered us the day before. On arriving at the fields, they lay in ambush about two hours, but saw no Indians. They then proceeded to follow a trail that was discovered the evening before—pursued the trail about two hours—came upon a camp—*surprised and took prisoners ten women and children*, and *accidentally shot one woman*—mistaking her for a warrior. The women say *the warriors were absent hunting*. In re-assembling my command at Fort Andrews on the 3rd of June, I found seventy-one men on the sick report; and though the well men were ready to continue operations, I judged it more prudent, after twenty-six days of severe labor and exposure, to march them to their separate camps, to repair their health and strength.

We have, on this scout, broke up four encampments of Indians, which must have contained from 125 to 150, old and young; and it is reasonable to suppose that we did not find all.

A

NARRATIVE

OF THE

LIFE AND SUFFERINGS

OF

MRS. JANE JOHNS,

WHO WAS BARBAROUSLY WOUNDED AND SCALPED BY
SEMINOLE INDIANS, IN EAST FLORIDA.

A NARRATIVE

OF THE

LIFE AND SUFFERINGS

OF

MRS. JANE JOHNS,

WHO WAS BARBAROUSLY WOUNDED AND SCALPED BY SEMINOLE INDIANS, IN EAST FLORIDA.

"Every man *shall give* as he is able, according to the blessing of the Lord thy God, which he hath given thee."—*Deut.* 16. xvii.

PUBLISHED EXCLUSIVELY FOR HER BENEFIT.

CHARLESTON:
PRINTED BY BURKE & GILES,
NO. 1 QUEEN-STREET.
1837.

ENTERED according to Act of Congress, in the Clerk's Office of the District Court of South-Carolina.

TO THE REV. DAVID BROWN,
RECTOR OF TRINITY CHURCH,
St. Augustine, East Florida.

Sir,

Your benevolent and charitable exertions to relieve the sufferings of the unhappy young widow, Mrs. Johns, by your timely and eloquent appeal to the sympathies of your congregation, have called forth her warmest gratitude and the general praise of your Christian brethren.

Permit me, Sir, in testimony of your worth, and in thankfulness for the valuable addition you have been pleased to make to this humble design, to dedicate to you these few pages.

That you may long live in the enjoyment of your health, and that peace of mind which ever attends upon the truly pious, is the sincere wish of

Your devoted servant,
THE WRITER.

East Florida, Feb. 4, 1837.

PREFACE.

The writer, in publishing this Narrative, is guided in his undertaking solely by a desire to benefit the unfortunate object herein referred to. Circumstances incidental to the early life of Mrs. Johns, were received from her aunt, Mrs. Carter, (a lady much respected in Florida) who constituted one of the suffering refugees from Trout Creek to Pearson's Island. Those facts which relate to Mrs. J's. being shot and scalped, have already been before the public through the newspapers, and are so well authenticated, as to preclude a doubt of their correctness.—Vide Appendix B.

The address to Dr. Welch would not have been annexed, but that it brings with it corroborative evidence of the respectable character which Mrs. Johns hitherto sustained in Florida. It is not probable that such distinguished gentlemen as Col. Mills, Col. Dell, His Honor Judge Doggett, and in fact any of the subscribers to the handsome letter to Dr. Welch, would have lent their names upon such an occasion, were they not convinced that Mrs. Johns merited the sympathy of the public.—Vide Appendix C.

Any further appeal than the plain statement of the sufferings of Mrs. Johns, would not only be useless, but an absolute innovation upon the better judgment of public feeling. It is sufficient that the community be in possession of this simple narrative, and the writer feels well assured it cannot be perused without commiserating the deep afflictions of the destitute young person for whose benefit it is designed.

NARRATIVE.

CHAPTER I.

In the records of Indian warfare, a more interesting case of extreme suffering, singular adventure, and wonderful escape from the hands of savages, has probably never occurred, than in that of the unfortunate subject of the following narrative. Many have been the victims who have fallen beneath the tomahawk, or before the Indian arrow or rifle; of these some have been scalped after, and some undoubtedly before life became extinct; but few have survived the combined effects of the rifle, the scalping knife and fire, as occurred in the case of the young lady, whose sufferings we are now about to detail.

The parents of Mrs. Johns occupied a respectable station in East Florida, and had, previous to incursions of the Indians, accumulated a sufficiency of worldly goods to render them comfortably independent. It appears they were pious and contented Christians, floating easily down the tranquil stream of life, to the year 1813, when they were first aroused from their sweet repose of peace and quiet, by the fierce yell of the savage sons of the forest. Here commenced the first act of Indian tragedy, in which this worthy family bore a conspicuous part, and in which (although then in *embryo*) Jane was an unconscious participator.

At this period, Mr. and Mrs. Hall, the father and mother of the present Mrs. Johns, dwelt upon the borders of Trout Creek, which empties itself into the superb river St. John, when the whole of this district became devastated by Seminole Indians, who appeared in a considerable body in the immediate neighborhood of their residence. Mr. and Mrs. H. fled at night, but only in time to hear the wailings and lamentations of their friends and neighbors, many of whom were sacrified; among them, were James Hollingsworth and Daniel Pritchard, whose scalps were subsequently presented to the Spanish Commandant in St. Augustine, who paid a premium to the Indians for such horrid and disgusting trophies.

From the vicinity of this dreadful massacre, the parents of Mrs. Johns escaped in a boat, and fled to Pearson's Island, on the sea coast, a distance of about fifty miles.

The sufferings of Mrs. Hall at this time must have been very great, exposed as she was, in an open boat, to the alternate effects of heavy rains and a scorching sun, for many hours, in a very enfeebled state of health—and scarcely had these unfortunate people landed upon this hitherto uninhabited and desolate Island, than Mrs. H. was warned by nature that an addition would be made to its population. A bench was hastily formed of such boards as could be procured from the boat which had conveyed them hither, raised sufficiently high to keep Mrs. H. from the wet earth; and upon this rude construction, with no other canopy than that of heaven, was the unfortunate subject of this narrative ushered into a world of trial and trouble, August 23d, 1813.

As speedily as possible after this sudden event, a tenement was formed of the bark of pine trees and palmetto leaves, in which the family resided from August to the succeeding January.

CHAPTER II.

Confidence being again restored, Mr. and Mrs. Hall returned to within a few miles of where they formerly dwelt, and settled upon a wild romantic spot called "Sweet Water Branch." Here they remained until April 16, 1821, when this persecuted family were again startled from their tranquile by the appalling war-whoop, to them doubly terrific from the painful associations of past events. A second time did they escape, hurrying with them little Jane, now in her eighth year. In this attack, her brother fell by the hands of the merciless savage, and her uncle received three desperate wounds from their unerring rifles—one ball fractured his arm, a second passed through his leg, and a third through the hip-bone. Again were the ears of these persecuted people assailed by the dying shrieks of their expiring neighbors, for they distinctly heard the vain screams and cries for help of two young ladies, and their mother (Mrs. Lane) who were then being butchered by Indians.

Screened from the keen eyes of their barbarous enemies by the mantle of darkness, saying in the language of Scripture, "Come let us return unto the Lord, for he hath torn and he will heal us; he hath smitten and he will bind us up"—they now sought refuge on the eastern side of the river St. John, where sickness succeeded their recent afflictions, and the family consequently removed to the vicinity of St. Mary's river, and there remained until peace was once more arranged between the red and white man. Mr. Hall and his family then retired into the interior, and established a farm at Alachua, upon the banks of New River—here Miss Jane Hall remained until her marriage, which took place in January, 1836. She now became the wife of Mr. Clement Johns, a young man of excellent character and of industrious habits. The first essay in life of this young couple, was to rent a farm, and were in the way of obtaining a comfortable maintenance, when they were suddenly and unexpectedly surrounded by Indians.

As corroborating testimony of the courage, suffering, and almost unprecedented preservation of Mrs. Johns from death, and escape from the hands of a more than brutal foe, we will take a statement of the circumstances relative to this horrible epoch in the life of Mrs. Johns, as related in the Journal of Dr. Andrew Welch, Post Surgeon to the Military Station at the city of Jacksonville, East Florida.

CHAPTER III.

Extract from the Journal of Dr. Welch.

"On Saturday, Sept. 17, 1836, I was requested by a committee, formed of the most respectable inhabitants of this city (Jacksonville), to visit Mrs. Johns, who, it was reported on good authority, had recently been dangerously wounded and scalped by Indians. I immediately complied.

"Although at the convocation of this meeting, Volunteers were numerous to form an escort, their number gradually subsided to five, viz.: Captain John L. Thigpen, and privates Granville and George Priest, brothers, (the younger about 16 years of age), John Faulk and Frederick Miller. Under this guard, accompanied by a carriage and driver belonging to Col. James Dell, supplied with that promptitude and humane feeling for which he is so justly celebrated, I proceeded for the purpose of rendering Mrs. Johns such aid as my humble skill could afford, and if possible, to bring back in the carriage to Jacksonville, the wretched sufferer, where she would be in less danger than in the vicinity of her late home.

"The day was far advanced before our departure—nor had we progressed beyond three miles, when Miller commenced a frivolous excuse and finally deserted, leaving only four and myself to fulfil our melancholy and certainly hazardous duty.

"We halted for the night at Mr. Eubank's plantation, from whence the enemy had taken some horses a few nights previous.

"*Sept.* 18.—Early this morning we proceeded by an unfrequented trail through the dreary and monotonous pine forest, until we arrived at the still burning embers of the fire which had consumed the greater portion of the body of poor Mr. Johns.

"The house in which he and his affectionate young wife had so lately dwelt in all the bliss of early wedded love, was now nought but a few smouldering ruins, in the centre of which a few bricks pointed out the spot where lied buried, a portion only, of the remains of one who but a few days since, lived in health and high hope of reaping the fruits of his honest labor—the surrounding cultivation showed evidence of his industry and enterprise.

"Never did I behold a more melancholy or wilder scene than that on which I now gazed in sadness—in one spot I saw some calcined human bones left unsepulchred, being too fragile to remove—they pulverized at the touch. In another place, I noticed fragments of glasses, plates, and other articles of domestic use, from which, but a few hours previous, this fond young couple had received in thankfulness, their daily sustenance—upon the stump of a pine tree I found some remains of hair—here the murderous villains had severed from the scalp of the yet living young widow, her long, and lately so much admired tresses.

"Some fifteen or twenty minutes were spent in sorrowful contemplation, reviewing this sylvan scene of death and desolation, when I was startled from deep reverie by the brief command—mount—which burst from the lips of our Captain, seemingly by an effort to give vent to a heart crowded by feelings of grief and indignation. In melancholy mood we now quitted this, never to be forgotten, wilderness.

"Our route now passed through some dangerous situations for ambuscade, and I could but admire the caution and discretion on the part of Capt. Thigpen on these occasions, in warning his men of the necessity of strict silence and vigilance—at the same time impressing upon them the importance of our undertaking. Although Major Hart had passed but a few days previous with a large company of men, our small band was at great risk of falling in with straggling Indians, who (as has been since proved,) were still lurking in this vicinity.

"About twelve miles from the late scene of human butchery brought us to the residence of Mr. Sparkman, under whose hospitable roof Mrs. Johns had been conveyed. Merciful God! and to his mercy alone can be attributed the strength which enabled this child of sorrow to travel this distance under such a complication of wounds and afflictions.

"Here I beheld a sight, at the bare recollection of which my very heart sickens. I until then thought I had viewed, in the course of my professional career, wounds of the most revolting character. I have witnessed many horrors in the practice of surgery, I might almost venture to acknowledge without wincing—but when I looked upon this young widow, prostrate, in calm resignation, with one arm deeply lacerated, so much so that the muscles absolutely gaped open nearly to the bones. The same rifle ball which had effected this wound passed through the neck; these, in themselves, were painful to behold in one so peculiarly wretched, but who can depict in colors sufficiently powerful to convey to the imagination the appalling spectacle of her head, divested of the scalp to the bare bone, in two places of which it was not only denuded and scraped, but portions absolutely cut out by the knife of the demon who had inflicted such unheard of torture!!! I measured the extent of skull divested of its natural integuments, which was, from the upper part of the forehead (leaving at its commencement only a few hairs,) to the occiput, nine inches and a half—from above one ear to the opposite, nine inches—on the right side of the head it appeared to me that the knife had slipped, a cut had been made obliquely, otherwise the circumcision of the scalp was tolerably regular. Her legs were considerably burned, but not to the extent I apprehended, from the appearance of her dress when shewn to me.

"Mrs. Johns was at this time thoroughly sensible of her situation, with a perfect recollection of all the circumstances connected with this piteous tragedy.

"The following morning I submitted to her choice whether to proceed with me to Jacksonville, where, if she should arrive, every necessary for her could be readily procured, and where she would be in comparative safety—or remain in her present situation, where a probability existed of her dying for want of surgical assistance. My professional duties in Jacksonville precluded the possibility of my being detained any length of time. Observing in her a character for resolution and determination, I unhesitatingly pointed out all the difficulties by which we were surrounded. I went so far as to express an apprehension that we might be attacked on our road to Jacksonville, or that she might perish on the way by fatigue and exposure. On the other hand, should the Indians be informed that she was still in existence, the house in which she then was, would in all likelihood be assailed. She deliberated a few minutes and then firmly decided to proceed with me. I felt much relieved by her determination."

CHAPTER IV.

Continuation of Dr. Welch's Narrative.

"Taking a different route from that by which we came, for some miles we progressed slowly, the carriage at times passing over logs and through swamps and ravines—she must have suffered dreadfully but did not complain.

"Captain Thigpen now pointed out certain signs which he assured me were those left by Indians, and he presently became confirmed in his belief, by discovering at a distance a fire—in so unfrequented a spot, (in time of war,) and in a section of country known to be infested by savages, he said he felt assured that the enemy was at hand. Capt. T—, George Priest, and myself reconnoitred as far as was consistent with safety or without discovering ourselves, and thereby exposing the life of our interesting charge to great hazard. We returned to the carriage in some anxiety—Mrs. Johns was aware of the danger by which we were threatened, but appeared resigned and passive. I do firmly believe that every man of our little escort would sooner have perished than abandon our patient protegée—happily we passed on unmolested, and after a tedious journey of eleven hours, arrived at Jacksonville.

My patient was much exhausted, but taking into consideration her enfeebled state of body from loss of blood, consequent upon the dreadful cruelties inflicted upon her—her extreme mental suffering, and her being at the same time near the period of parturition—it becomes a matter of wonder how she was supported in such an undertaking."

Mrs. Johns continued in a feeble state until Oct. 6th, when, in addition to all her former sufferings, her last and fondest hope was blighted. By the kindest care and attention, the mother was saved from death, but nature could not sustain such an accumulation of trials,—her infant had perished some days previous to her confinement.

The following notice in the Jacksonville Courier was taken of this event:

"Mrs. Jane Johns, who was so barbarously scalped a short time since in this vicinity, is convalescing rapidly—her sufferings have been extreme, though much relieved by the praiseworthy attention and skill of Dr. Andrew Welch.

"The 6th ult., Mrs. Johns gave birth to a still born child."

CHAPTER V.

We think it necessary to pursue the statement of circumstances attendant upon the murder of Mr. Johns, and the wounding and scalping of Mrs. J., as received from her subsequent to her arrival in Jacksonville—viz:

"On Thursday morning, about 10 o'clock, Mr. and Mrs. Johns discovered Indians at the corner of a fence, within a few yards of where they then stood. No sooner had they clearly discovered their war-painted enemies, than three rifles were discharged; the last took effect in the breast of the early doomed husband—both fled to the house as fast as the tottering limbs of poor wounded Johns would permit, who was bleeding profusely. On gaining the house, Mrs. J. closed the door. Here was exhibited the first act of courage and devotion by this fond young wife—unheeding her own danger, or thinking of self-preservation, she carefully tied a handkerchief round the body of her husband, hoping to stay the rapid effusion of blood! What must have been the state of her feelings at this critical moment? her husband evidently mortally wounded—no friend to counsel or cheer her—and nine blood thirsty savages approaching her insecure retreat.

"The Indians cautiously advanced near and nearer still, until Mrs. Johns saw them peering through the cracks of their log-built cottage, which being newly erected, were sufficiently wide for her to distinguish clearly a considerable portion of the faces of these terrific hyenas. She counted nine: among them was a negro, who joined the Indians in urging Mr. and Mrs. Johns to leave the house, threatening, if they did not, it should be immediately set fire to.

"Mr. Johns, during this time, was seated on one end of a table—he took his rifle, threw away the former priming, intending to renew it with fresh powder, but became, as Mrs. Johns supposes, too weak to complete his design. Both now piteously entreated the hell-hounds would spare their lives. This appeal only served to convince the Indians of their own safety in the entire helplessness of their victims. An order was now issued to *charge the house*, which mandate was delivered in good English, and immediately complied with. The door was burst open, and Mr. Johns, in an instant shot through the brain.

"The frantic young wife, in an agony of grief, desirous to receive a death-blow that should consign them both to one early grave, threw herself upon the bleeding corpse of her husband. An Indian now seized her by the hand, and dragged her with violence to the door, saying, in his own language, *hie pelon eschay*—go. She demanded to where? And he pointed in a Westerly direction. Before she could even cast "one longing, lingering look behind," another Indian presented his rifle at her head; she intuitively held up her arm, through which a ball instantly passed; then through the neck. Mrs. J. observes, she noticed a grin of delight upon the countenance of the Indian who shot her. In relating this horrible adventure she says, she did not feel hurt, but fell. Clinging to a forlorn hope, she feigned death; laying with her face upon her hands, she beheld distinctly the monster in his infernal preparation for scalping her. He first took from her head, her comb, and loosed her flowing hair. He then stepped back a few feet, and drew from his side a common wooden handle butcher's knife, which to her mind, she remarks, rendered it doubtful whether designed for her throat, or for their customary, and last operation after death—*scalping*.

She remained, as if already dead, until he left her, with his disgusting trophy.

"He had strip'd the flesh,
As ye peal the fig when the fruit is fresh."

CHAPTER VI.

It seems the next object of the savages was to set fire to the house, and although there was a tolerable fire at the moment in the room, Mrs. Johns heard one Indian desire another to strike a light,* which being done, a blaze was produced, and some dried fodder in a loft above the room ignited. A torch was next applied to her dress, at the feet; she had sufficient presence of mind and fortitude even to allow the flesh of her lower extremities to burn, until the Indians left the premises, which they now did in much haste, making the welkin ring with their war-whoop.

From the moment of Mrs. Johns being scalped, the Indians were necessitated to pass by her body repeatedly, and as she lay partly in one room, and partly in the passage which passed through the centre of the building, they had some difficulty in their ingress and egress, without coming in actual contact with her person, which they now seemed to shun with horror or disgust.†

---

* From some superstitious belief, Indians do not use the fire which has been kindled by white men, for the destruction of their property, but always have recourse to that procured by themselves.—*Related by Mrs. Carter, aunt to Mrs. Johns, who lived many years in close vicinity to the Indians in Florida.*

† Indians, after touching the corpse of a pregnant woman, consider themselves unclean until they have performed ablutions, and purified themselves with physic

Finding all quiet, her first thought was to extinguish the fire of her clothes, to accomplish which, she scraped the blood from her denuded head in her hands, and cautiously (for she still feared some Indians were near) applied it to the fire, which was actually consuming her.

After having extinguished the fire of her dress, she raised herself up, but immediately fainted. On recovering, her first object was to remove the body of her husband, to prevent its being consumed by the devouring element, which was making rapid progress through the roof. In this humane and affectionate design, she was defeated by want of physical strength. Being convinced of her incapacity to remove the corpse, she attempted her own escape, and no sooner had she reached the outside of the house, than she again became senseless. Once more restored to reason, she noticed a bag, in which coffee had been kept; this she applied to her bare skull, to defend it from the piercing rays of the sun, which at this time poured down its effulgent beams with cruel effect.

In this deplorable condition, she crawled (after repeatedly fainting) a distance of about 200 yards, to a shallow pond of water, and after slaking her thirst, from her hands, deeply imbrued in her own gore, she laid herself down, as she supposed, to die.

Her chief object in going so far, she observes, was with a view of preventing the Indians discovering her retreat, apprehending she might be immolated upon the burning pile consuming her doubly murdered husband. At the same time, she was impressed with an idea, that should she die in her present situation, her body might be discovered by some friend, whose attention would be roused by the buzzards, which would soon be hovering around her.

Four or five hours must have passed away in a state of partial unconsciousness before Mrs. Johns was discovered. She lifted up her voice in prayer, and the Father of mercies heard her supplications. She cried unto the Lord,

"The enemy hath persecuted my soul, he hath smitten my life down to the ground; he hath made me to dwell in darkness, as those that have been long dead."

"Therefore is my spirit overwhelmed within me; my heart within me is desolation."

---

and sweating. The latter is performed by digging holes in the earth, into which they bury themselves to the chin.—*Ibid*.

CHAPTER VI.

This desolate young woman had now drained the cup of misery to its last and bitterest dregs—the lamp of life was fast flickering—she says that all appeared black before her—true indeed, "*she dwelt in darkness.*"

In this "extremity of earthly woe" was she discovered by ——, her lost husband's father! who was returning from Black Creek, accompanied by his friend and neighbour, Mr. Lowther. Well might they have exclaimed with Shakespeare,

> "Art thou any thing?
> Art thou some God, some Angel or some Devil,
> That makest my blood cold and my hair to stand?
> Speak to me, what art thou?"

We leave the reader to figure to himself the agonizing position of these two gentlemen when they first caught sight of the still blazing habitation from whence Mr. Johns had three days previous parted from his son and daughter-in-law, (to whom he was equally attached,) and Mr. Lowther having left a family within seven miles (the nearest residence) of this scene of annihilation.

Both immediately knew, by evidence of tracks and other signs, (readily distinguished, by inland settlers,) that Indians had here exercised their revengeful ravages. Their first impression was, that the young pair had shared an equal fate in the conflagration; something was now observed moving in the water at some paces distant; each carefully approached, until Mr. Johns declared it at first to be an Indian, and then an Indian squaw with a red handkerchief upon her head. Under this impression, yielding to the phrenzied feeling of a bereaved parent, he raised his rifle to his shoulder, determined upon some satisfaction from (as he supposed,) one of his enemies, when Mr. Lowther, with that humanity which does honor to his nature, entreated him to forbear, and not to take away the life of a defenceless woman. He remembered that "*The Lord is merciful and gracious, slow to anger, and plenteous in mercy.*"

This natural ebulition of spirit in Mr. Johns became allayed, and in some measure pacified—both advanced to within a few feet of the object before them, when, how much greater must have been their horror and amazement to discover that the helpless creature was not an enemy, but the scarcely living daughter-in-law of him who had been on the verge of extinguishing her remaining feeble spark of life.

In addition to her misfortunes already enumerated, Mrs. Johns, on January 17th, 1837, lost her father, who died at Black Creek, after having experienced the entire loss of his property by Indians, which, with the sufferings of his child, it is presumed, hastened him to his eternal place of rest. Thus is this young widow, (trained to every expectation of ease and comfort) at the early age of twenty-three years, deprived of her last and only stay for support—consequently, at the earnest persuasion of her friends, calls upon a generous public for sympathy and succor—both in behalf of herself and an aged mother.

APPENDIX.

(A.)

Annexed are some passages of a sermon preached by the Rev. David Brown in St. Augustine, November 1836—on the occasion of a collection for the most unfortunate Mrs. Johns.

"My daughter is even now dead; but come and lay thy hand upon her, and she shall live.—Matt. ix. 18.

The text, as falling in our way in to-day's service,* is adapted, rather as an appropriate *motto*, than as a foundation of discourse. * * * And Jesus arose and followed the afflicted suppliant, and so did his disciples. And when he came into the ruler's house, amid the jeers and scoffs of the unfeeling bystanders—mourners by trade—who laughed him to scorn, he approached to lay the hand of his healing power upon her. The sufferers were put forth, and he took her by the hand and she arose. And the father's heart, stricken and torn, and crushed, as it had been, was gladdened with joy, that his darling was restored. * * * * * *
I am to speak of those who have known all the mystery of death, but who can speak of that sublime subject only from the grave! *Of one*, and for one, I am to speak, from whose bloody couch of pain and mutilation, much we might learn of death's mysterious character and doings! She was snatched from his last grasp by her protecting angel, that she might give lessons of thought to the unthinking, and teach, if any thing can, the unfeeling heart of apathy, that "feels no sorrows but its own," to throb with sympathy for others woes.

And *to* those I am to speak who are *bound*, in all reason bound, to think deeply and soberly on the condition and on the signs of the times; and who strongly should *feel* that sober thought and active virtue become their condition and prospects, as citizens of a suffering—perhaps a doomed country;—as candidates for another state of being, where ere long all the mysteries of death will be also known.

*Twenty-fourth Sunday after Trinity.

It is not my intention, nor has it ever been, to *amuse*, but to *benefit* my hearers. It has never been mine to seek the poor meed of popular applause, generally despicable in itself, and most often awarded to despicable displays of common place declamation, equally foreign from correct taste and from divine truth; of influence alone, with such as could be influenced by nothing better—stony hearts and vacant heads. To hearts which can *feel*, and to heads that can *think*, I would now address myself. Such I shall not fail to interest; for they will go with me where there is every thing to move the feeling heart and to engage the deep thoughts of every sober mind. And surely, this bleeding country's hearts and minds should feel and think intensely and deeply. It is meet, and right, and their bounden duty. The means too, as well as the cause, are at hand, in the desolations and diseases, and in blood; and in bereavements of every character, every where presented to our view. In our streets, the maimed and the war stricken; in our hospitals and homes, the disabled and dying are found in numbers, calling on us for sympathy and for succor.

Ask some maimed one, yet spared the blessed privilege to move, to accompany you to where, in your own city, rest in the silent grave, the brave unfortunate youths, whose young blood has moistened the soil of our country!

When he has told you, how boldly, and how bitterly, they fought, and fell, and suffered—lingering out many days and nights in anguish—hear then the especially sad tale of one, in beauteous early manhood, whom twice spared, as by a miracle, from a watery grave, was brought down by a savage rifle, to suffer a long agony of pain, ere he fell into an untimely grave, soon to be followed by a broken hearted mother.*

My friends, do you know any thing of the meaning of a broken heart?

She felt, in the loss of her darling son, by a death so shocking, that the hand of the "great and the dreadful God" was upon her, and with her heart crushed under it, she shrieked, and shrank into the grave.

Was she *alone*, in this extremity of suffering? No brethren! she was but an example before your eyes, of a large class of extreme sufferers, in our suffering land by this savage war.

In her case, the silver cord of life was broken too,—in mercy broken—and death came to her sad relief! And many more are still *living* examples of broken heartedness. Well may the tear fall on the graves of the youthful warriors, who fell in mortal conflict, but lingered in life to be buried among their friends, and on the graves too, of those unhappy ones from far—denied the blessed privilege to die among their friends—who sleep with strangers. They are tears that warm the heart. But what is there to warm, or to soothe

---

*Domingo Martinelly, died of his wounds received at Dunlawton; and his mother died as stated above.

in the recollection of his severer fate, who was left in full health to perish—none can tell the manner. The shocked soul recoils from the contemplation.* And rich is the grace, and powerful as rich, which has sustained the mother, so stricken and bereaved, by that dire and mysterious calamity.

But in the thoughts of *His* chastisements, who never willingly afflicts, shall we forget his remembered mercy? No! Let the shocked soul still expand in grateful acknowledgment, that the brave survivors of the youthful victims alluded to were saved from the dreadful fate of a far stronger body of brave men. That Putnam is not another Dade, and Dunlawton another field of savage massacre, not one escaping to tell the tale of woe. God be praised for all his mercies!   *   *   *   *   *   *   *   *

It is a declaration of wisdom, that it is better for the heart to go to a house of mourning, than to a house of mirth. It must then be profitable for us to soften our hearts by a recollection of some of the sad events, which have brought distress and mourning upon our land.

Little it is at most, that we can know—a small portion, perhaps, that we can imagine, of the amount of wretchedness, and grief and broken heartedness, which has already accumulated, and is still accumulating upon us, and diffusing its bitterness through the homes and hearts of our nation, to its utmost bounds.

Our imagination may very truly and vividly, bring before our view the deserted and bloody battle ground, where more than one hundred brave men, coming to our defence, were slain by the unsparing foe! Send forth your mind's eye and behold the dreadful panorama of Death! See the advance guard, and the gallant chief, cut down by the first fire of the enemy! Look on the ensuing, protracted, murderous conflict! Hear the savage yells, the crack, the crash, the volley, the roar, the groans and shrieks of the wounded and the dying! Orders, and spirit stirring words of courage, issuing from bleeding lips of maimed and mangled officers, to men not less maimed and mangled—the still living fragment of a late hale and gallant band!! Confusion reigns, and its kindly, though dreadful influence, gives relief to our lacerated hearts! We would revive their wholesome sympathies.

Select then a single object of contemplation. Let it be the young officer whose left arm is broken in the very beginning of the fight. For hours behold him, while still cheering the men, using the lacerated stump as a rest for his ever active musket, until he is finally overcome and slain! Or, to some hearts, a more affecting sight may be that of another, not less brave and devoted, *both* arms disabled, sitting on the ground, and, in mute and broken spirited amazement, gazing vacantly on the scene of horror and suffering that surrounds him. Oh! of all ruins, how most melancholy is that of the warm heart and the radiant brain! and especially by means so horrible.

---

*Information has since been received, that the lamented young man, Gould, was taken after the battle of Dunlawton, and shot by the Indians.

Or, again, the work of death seems finished! All, save ever and anon, a dying shriek. All is silent! The savage foe has retired! Satisfied with what he has done, he seems to respect the repose of the dying and the dead; when lo, the approach of a troop of deeply darker fiends to triumph over a fallen foe, which living they had not dared to face!

While they are employed in the coward work of butchering alike the dying and the dead, there comes forth bleeding and mangled from among the heaps of bloody corses, the last surviving officer—the gallant Bassinger. This soul of chivalry had never dreamed of beings in human form, who could resist the plea for life, at such a time, and under circumstances so deeply moving. Alas! his imploring wounds and supplicating lips avail not!

With fiend-like laughter, they reply to his prayer for life, and with the crimsoned axe the murderous scene is closed!

Ah! would *God*, in this cruel instance had stood alone, a solitary witness, that

"The angel Pity, shuns the walks of war."

All these scenes of woe, with many more, scarcely less dreadful and appalling, that might be named, however, give but a partial view of the real amount of misery produced by this savage war.

Our strong emotions are excited by the carnage of the battle field, and by the fate of the unsuspecting victim fallen under the ambushed foe! A mother with her infant children are murdered by a band of cruel ingrates. A husband and father is taken, and leaves a weeping widow and helplesss orphans to the world's cold charity. Thousands are driven from their hard earned homes of comfort, all to suffer; and many to perish by famine and pestilence; and we forget the distant tears that flow, and the far away hearts that are crushed by the feeling, that it is the survivor's self who dies!

Much is the *blood*, but more are the tears of anguish, which cry from the ground against the authors of this war! "Father, forgive them!" and oh! let thy consoling grace and mercy be vouchsafed to the widows and the orphans it has made; and to the bereaved parents and other relatives and friends, whose hearts it has sunk in sorrow, and whose eyes it has dimmed with weeping; and hasten thou on, the blessed day, when wars shall cease, and thy reign be established forever.   *   *   *   *   *   *   *

But, brethren and friends, on this occasion we are particularly to present to your notice the claims on your sympathy and kindness, of the greatly unfortunate woman for whose benefit a collection has been invited.

The case of Mrs. John's is one than which none can be named, or scarcely imagined, more powerfully adapted to warm the heart in sympathy, or in charity to open the liberal hand.

Her claims before us are made by a worthy and accredited representative of those who have suffered all that human nature can suffer and live. You are aware that she was despited of all but life; and even for that to the ruthless spoilers she is not indebted.

The crumbling bones, found by the pursuers of the foe, among the ashes of her demolished home, were the bones of her doubly murdered husband! The blood stains were of their mingled gore! The hair steeped in blood and covered with dust and ashes, near the mouldering pile of ruin was from her own mangled head!

You require not to be told, that a severe wound from an Indian rifle was the tender mercy she obtained by supplicating the cruel savage; nor that the barbarian scalping knife was not withheld!

Left for dead, by the miscreant butchers, the fire kindling upon her garments aroused her from a death-like swoon, and with the blood of her own wounds having extinguished her burning garments, she attempted in vain to remove the remains of her murdered husband. Her almost exhausted strength but sufficed to carry her own bleeding and lacerated frame, from the consuming element.

Wretched, mutilated, and forlorn, she was found by the bereaved and sorrowing father of her dead partner, and removed to where she found shelter and kindness. From that shelter, and that kindness, her case required that she should be removed to where she would be within reach of medical aid; and even with the best helps which skill and kindness might afford, there remained but the slightest hope of her recovery.

But it has pleased God, in rich mysterious mercy, to preserve her through her perils, thus far; and it is believed she will recover, a living witness of the most ferocious barbarism.

God's healing hand has been laid upon her, and she lives!! * * Almost as from the dead she has risen, and I trust that none will be asked to contribute to her sustenance and comfort, who shall not deem it a privilege to be allowed thus to become a co-worker with God, by whom she has been rescued from a complicated death.

As all readers of the scriptures are acquainted with the obligatory and the rewardable character of the virtue to which you are now called, I need not dwell on the high and holy, and humane motives of the practice of it. It is too, an act of pure religion, and undefiled before God and the Father, that you are invited; for the object is indeed a widow in affliction, helpless and dependant, and to all who extend kindly the helping hand to her relief, I am authorized in saying, they "shall not lose their reward."

"Deal thy bread to the hungry, and bring the poor that are cast out, to thy house; then shall thy light break forth as the morning, and thine health spring forth speedily." * * * * *

(B.)

Extract from the Jacksonville Courier.
INDIANS—BUTCHERY—PURSUIT—ESCAPE.

Our townsmen who went day before yesterday to the rescue of Mr. Higginbotham's family, as stated in our last, have just returned—themselves and horses jaded and looking as if they had had a hard pursuit. They are the best and bravest of our men, and went with the expectation and determination to pursue and overtake and destroy these daring Indians.

Major Hart, to whom we are indebted for the following particulars, reports, that on Thursday about 10 o'clock, they reached the house of Mr. Higginbotham, which was attacked. There they found the two men (one of whom was sick) and the two ladies on guard with guns in their hands. The Indians had not re-appeared after their being beaten off before Mr. Higginbotham left to report to us in town. On a slight examination, they saw a number of bullet marks in the house, made by the Indian's shots—and saw the clothes of the younger lady, through which a rifle ball had passed. She had arisen early, and gone out towards a branch for water, when the attack was made upon the house, between which and herself were the Indians. The Indians fired at her, and one ball passed her side so close as to cut through *all* her clothes, but touched not her body. She ran to the branch, secreting herself therein, and subsequently made her way into the house, past the Indians in safety. After a little time, spent in search, the party under Maj. Hart found where the Indians encamped the night previous, not three-fourths of a mile from the house, and also the spot where the horses were tied while the attack was made on the house. From that spot our party took the Indians' trail. It struck the Tallahassee road, and these daring devils kept the road for near 10 miles, riding at full speed as their trail showed, till they came to Mr. M'Cormick's house, then occupied by Mr. Johns and wife, on the road 18 miles from Jacksonville. Our party in pursuit reached this house about 4 o'clock P. M. It was a mouldering pile of ruins. On examination, Major Hart states, that they found the calcined bones of a human *being burned* in the house. A piece of the *back bone* was found with *some flesh upon it*. The skull was to be seen, but at the touch it fell in and crumbled to pieces. The bones were mostly reduced to ashes. Near the house was found a quantity of hair, to appearance that of a female. Thence the trail seemed to be still on the road, and our men pushed on with increased speed and anxiety, to overtake the murdering Indians. They expected to do so at the next house, (Mr. Lowder's) 7 miles ahead. On arriving there they found the house abandoned by the two females and their children who lived there, but unvisited by the Indians. The inmates had evidently fled in alarm, as the dinner they were preparing was still at the fire and warm, of which our party partook—and then, doubtful of the trail they were on, set out for Mr. Sparkman's, 4 miles distant. It was after night when they reached Mr. Sparkman's, nor was it possible for them to determine whether they were on a trail or not. Great distress filled the house of Mr. Sparkman. There was Mrs. Johns—her arm laid open with a rifle bullet—a ball shot through her neck—and her scalp, so far as the hair extended over her head, most horribly and manglingly taken off—and *she still alive!!* Good God! who can hear the bare recital of such a deed, and not feel horror-stricken at the cold-blooded barbarity! Who can hear, and not feel a thirst to revenge such outrage?

She was able to state the circumstances of the attack upon herself and husband. They were about twenty yards from the house, between 10 and 11 o'clock Thursday morning, when the Indians showed themselves by the corner of a fence close to them. The Indians fired and wounded Mr. Johns in the left breast. Both ran for the house, entered and closed the door. The Indians came up and fired on the house. They called out in English, and told them if they would come out they should not be hurt. The Indians looked in through the cracks (the house was made of logs) and told Mr. Johns and his wife to come out; but they did not consent to do so, but begged for their lives. The order was given in English to charge the house. The Indians burst in—shot Mr. Johns through the head—he fell, and his wife fell upon his body. An Indian dragged her to the door, and said to her, "hi-e-pus-cha," "go." She asked where, and he pointed towards the head of Black Creek. At that moment she saw another Indian level his rifle—she threw up her arm—the Indian fired—and the ball, cutting lengthwise through the flesh of her arm, passed through her neck. She fell. The Indian came up—dragged her into the hall of the house (the house is what is called a double log-house) and then taking out her comb and tearing the string from her hair, *scalped her.* He did not tear the scalp off, but cut it as butchers take the skin from a beef. During this operation Mrs. Johns was sensible of what was doing. She saw the Indian's scalping-knife, and says it was a round pointed common butcher-knife. She lay as if dead. The Indians plundered the house, taking a pair of portmanteau containing money to some amount, and every thing of value—set fire to the house, and one Indian applied the torch to her clothes—left the house—gave a whoop, and hurried off in the direction, she thought from their noise, of the head of Black Creek. She felt the fire of her clothes upon one leg, and as soon as she dared to move so much, grabbed in her hand a quantity of her own clotted blood, with which she put out her burning clothes. And then, when the Indians were out of hearing, she got up—saw her murdered husband's body unscalped and unmoved from the position in which he fell, except the Indians had put one foot up on the edge of a table. The house was on fire—she made her way out of it, fainting every few minutes. She reached the edge of a swamp—got some water and there lay down, unable to get farther. There she remained till 2 o'clock P. M. when three men, Mr. Johns, the father of her husband, Mr. Lowder, and Mr. M'Kinney came along. They saw the burning house all fallen, in except the corners of the logs, the body therein burned—and discovered her, whom they took to be an Indian at first, then a squaw. On advancing to her, what must have been the feelings of her father-in-law, to recognize in the butchered, bloody, almost lifeless woman, his daughter-in-law—and to know that the burned human frame in the house was that of his son! These three men carried her to Mr. Lowder's, and giving the inmates of the house the alarm, and taking them, the two females and their children, went on to Mr. Sparkman's—where our party in pursuit of the Indians, found them as above stated.

It was the trail of these men that was mistaken for that of the Indians. The Indians were all mounted, and the trail was therefore easily mistaken. Mrs. Johns saw eight Indians and one negro—the negro was naked except a woollen flap he wore. She saw no horses and probably there were more than eight Indians, as they would undoubtedly be very likely to leave some with the horses. It was now ascertained that the Indians had taken five horses from Mr. Eubank, one from Mr. Ratcliff, and three from Mr. Johns, whom they murdered, and also that our party was off their trail. It was not possible to follow the trail of horses in the night, and therefore our men encamped. Early in the morning they set out, and supposing the Indians turned from the left of the road, they struck into the woods in order to come upon the trail without losing the time of retracing their steps to the house where Mr. Johns was burned. They struck the trail quite early and followed it with all the speed possible. They found where the Indians stopped to take a lunch as was supposed. They continued the pursuit to the head of Black Creek, where finding that the Indians, having, as was known, six hours the start on the day before, had travelled in the night, and that too, with great rapidity, as the trail showed, our townsmen, with those who joined them, making twenty in number, came to the conclusion that further pursuit would be useless, and with disappointment, and regret and reluctance, gave up the pursuit, and it being near night; on Friday they turned for home, and reached here to-day.

The Indians rode with all the speed of their horses. Those they took were among the best in our county, and able to bear pushing. Our party had good horses, and they pushed them in the pursuit all that their speed and bottom would bear, but it was in vain. The enemy expected pursuit, and therefore directed their rapid flight for the nation, where it is supposed they arrived without stopping. It is presumed they made for Payne's Prairie. We had hoped that this daring party would have been rash enough to attempt to drive cattle before them. In that case our men would have pushed on till they overtook them. These Indians came in the same direction they took on their return. There were plainly to be seen here and there the remnants of a trail, especially in the grass and by the palmetto leaves gathered in several places, where they stopped and probably encamped. It is thought they came in ten days or two weeks ago —during which time to the present they have been lurking about Brandy-Branch, where Indians have several times been seen. They have undoubtedly spied out this whole section and are now gone to report their intelligence, taking with them nine stolen horses and a woman's scalp. It is true this party of Indians were well mounted on fresh horses, but still the issue of the pursuit shows how almost impossible it is to overtake them in their retreat after committing depredations. If they have a few hours only the start, they can reach the nation in safety and mock pursuit. In truth a good portion of the movements of the army (there are some bright exceptions) have failed of effect through tardiness and through want of a sufficient number of good spies.

That these cursed butcherers, so bold as to come within seven miles to commit their depredations, should escape from so ready, rapid, and hot a pursuit, and that too, from men of known bravery and perseverance, and determined at every hazard to overtake and chastise them, gives us great mortification and pain. They did all that men could do, except running, only twenty strong, and without food and forage, into the nation after them, which would have been folly and rashness.

Upon the arrival at Black Creek of the express sent to Maj. Pierce, he immediately ordered out three companies in different directions to cut off their retreat. The Indians undoubtedly passed near Kingsley's Pond. We understand a company went to that pass on Friday evening, but saw neither Indians nor their trail. The companies returned Friday night without making any discoverd. We are informed that on Saturday morning Maj. Pierce, at the head of 50 men, went again to strike, if possible, their trail, in consequence of the report of the mail carrier from this place, who arrived Friday night. We pray that Maj. Pierce, to whom great credit is due for his prompt and vigorous exertions to intercept this banditti, may be able to fall in with them.

* * * * * * * *

Before an order could be issued by Capt. Blanchard, three of his men and two of Capt. Priest's sons volunteered as a guard to escort Mrs. Johns in. Dr. Welch readily volunteered his services as physician. This is the more creditable to Dr. W., as he was then the only physician in town. Col. Dell was laudably active in getting this assistance for Mrs. Johns. He sent his carriage, horse and driver to bring her in, if in the opinion of the physician her wounds would permit her removal. They set out immediately after the return of the company on Saturday. They returned on Monday evening, bringing Mrs. Johns, who endured the removal, a distance of thirty miles, with great fortitude.

It is enough to make the blood chill and rush painfully to the heart, to see this lady mangled as she is, and to think *how, when,* and *by whom* the deed was done. She is at Mr. Richard's. Every attention will be paid to her to render her distressed and unfortunate situation as comfortable as possible.

Capt. Thigpin who had command of this little escort, states that they saw Indian signs, and anticipated an attack. But all were determined to execute their mission or die in the attempt. They executed it with credit.

It is thought Mrs. Johns will recover.

(C.)

JACKSONVILLE, *January* 23d, 1837.

Dear Sir:—We, the undersigned, in behalf of the citizens of Jacksonville, and inhabitants of East Florida generally, do, with much respect, tender you our expression of admiration of your unwearied and kind attention in the exercise of your noble profession since you have dwelt among us; the exalted stand you have taken in Florida as a surgeon, and the urbanity of your deportment as a gentleman, claim our warmest sympathies.

Amongst the various opportunities offered for the exercise of your skill, two most remarkable cases have spread a "halo" around you, which must ever attract our lasting admiration and respect; we revert to the circumstances of John Pierson, whose shattered and ruined frame, you by firmness, promptitude, decision and perseverance, restored to health, although by the necessary sacrifice of his arm; and another still more remarkable instance of the wonders of the healing art has been recently evidenced by you in the cure of Mrs. Jane Johns; independent of our admiration for your professional abilities, you have claims in this instance upon the community, even of a more exalted character—it will not be readily effaced from the memories of the citizens of Jacksonville, the promptness with which you assented to a call for you to visit this bleeding sufferer, at a distance of thirty miles, through a portion of country known to be, at the time, infested by a cruel enemy, when all consideration of danger was set at nought by you, in the contemplation of your sacred duty; and when it was proposed to renumerate you for your services, you with that honest pride, which adds dignity and honor to the human character, rejected the proffered compensation. Not content with this instance of your worth and magnanimity, we are aware that your kindness, care, and unceasing attention to Mrs. Johns, for four months, has thus far been unrequited, except by the sweet reward of self-approval.

Circumstanced as this unfortunate young lady, Mrs. Johns, now is, bereft of her natural protector—her husband,—divested of all her property by fire, her peace of mind perhaps blighted forever, and her means of support entirely gone; we are of opinion that it will not only be beneficial to herself but gratifying to the public, that Mrs. Johns should yield to the urgent request of the citizens of Charleston to visit that city, that they may be convinced such statements as have already gone forth in relation to her having been scalped and otherwise dreadfully wounded, have not been exaggerated.

We cannot be surprised that doubt should have existed, her narrative being of so wonderful and tragical a nature.

As Mrs. Johns has not yet recovered from the shock her system has undergone, by such a complication of evils, as those which have recently attended her, and as it is her particular request, that she may longer enjoy the benefits of your skill and care, we venture to solicit, you will accompany her as her Physician and Surgeon.

We are aware of the sacrifice you must make, in abandoning a practice in which you have been so eminently successful, therefore, sir, permit us to insist, that you accept our promise of ample compensation, for this additional mark of your benevolence.

JAMES DELL.
W. J. MILLS.
JOHN L. DOGGETT.
J. D. HART.
EMORY RIDER.
H. R. BLANCHARD.
ROBERT BIGELOW.
D. S. GARDINER.
M. K. PINCKSTON.
H. H. PHILIPS.

ANDREW WELCH, M. D. Jacksonville.

DONATIONS will be thankfully received for Mrs. JOHNS, by

A NARRATIVE
OF THE LIFE OF
BENJAMIN BENSON.

A NARRATIVE

OF THE LIFE OF

BENJAMIN BENSON,

WHO WAS BORN A SLAVE IN THE

ISLAND OF BERMUDA,

EMANCIPATED BY THE ENGLISH GOVERNMENT, AUG. 1, 1838,

AND

SUBSEQUENTLY SOLD AS A SLAVE

IN THE

UNITED STATES OF AMERICA;

WITH A DETAIL OF HIS SEVERE TRIALS AND HARDSHIPS, AND CRUELTIES
INFLICTED UPON HIM BY HIS INHUMAN PERSECUTORS,

BY

ANDREW G. WELCH, M.D.,

AUTHOR OF "PRINCE ECONCHATTI;" "LIFE IN THE TIMBER," &c.

"My mind can reason, and my limbs can move
The same as yours—like yours my heart can love—
Alike my body food and sleep sustain,
And e'en like yours feel pleasure, want, and pain.
One sun rolls o'er us, common skies surround—
One globe contains us, and one grave must bound."

LONDON:
BY THE AUTHOR.
TO BE HAD OF ALL BOOKSELLERS.

1847.

TESTIMONIALS.

Dundee, 12th July, 1847.

I have read this narrative with much interest, an interest enhanced by the simple, clear, straight-forward manner in which it is told. It bears in every circumstance related, the stamp of truth; and I am nearly as certain that Benjamin Benson underwent, as that Dr. Welch has recorded, those adventures. Fervently do I trust that it may be instrumental in casting fresh light upon the sufferings of the abused and degraded negro race, and in exciting wider, and more accurate and profound sympathy in their favour.

GEORGE GILFILLAN.

Belfast, Aug. 20, 1847.

I have read Dr. Welch's narrative of the negro Benjamin Benson's eventful life: it has the fullest internal evidence of a truthful relation. To circulate such a narrative is the more useful, because it is no very singular story, but may go forth as the duplicate of many an injured, outraged, and fearfully wronged negro's destiny. Three millions of the family of Benson yet live to appeal to humanity for mitigation of their sufferings, and to the God of love for that compassion which men desire for themselves, but deny to the slave.

THOMAS DREW, D.D.

Belfast, 23rd Aug., 1847.

By the publication of the narrative of the life of Benjamin Benson, Dr. Welch has deserved the thanks of those who wait and labour for the overthrow of slavery.

The graphic picture of one slave's life and sufferings, does more to make the reader acquainted with the atrocity of the system, than the most profound and elaborate disquisitions on the evils of slavery. We are brought near to the features of the monster by such simple and touching recitals. Individual christians will pause and contemplate, and churches will feel the responsibility of encouraging such enormities.

What man in his most untutored state will do for freedom, may be learned from such biography, and the impossibility of crushing the love of liberty demonstrated. The sad reflection, however, must arise, how many such at this moment drink the bitter cup, whose tales have never been told, except in sighs, heard only by the God of Sabaoth! The truth of the narrative will not be doubted by those who are firmiliar with the condition of the slave,

ISAAC NELSON,
Presbyterian Minister.

PREFACE.

THERE can be no better means to arouse a sympathetic feeling for an oppressed people, than by selecting individual examples of injustice, and pourtraying them in true colours to the friends of freedom and humanity. Thus, by exciting a spirit of commisseration for the wrongs and sufferings of a few members, a benevolent feeling readily diffuses itself throughout the whole body similarly affected. With this view this little volume, with its numerous imperfections, is submitted to the perusal of the public.*

Although the editor does not pretend to any merit on the score of literary attainment, yet, from his having resid-

---

* The question is often mooted as to what influence the opinions of the English have upon the minds of the Americans? which may be best answered by a quotation from the "*Fifteenth Annual Report, presented to the Massachusetts Anti-Slavery Society, by its Board of Managers,*" January 27th, 1847:

"We borrow the manners, we copy the customs, we imitate the follies of the English. The question uppermost in most cis-Atlantic minds is that asked of Mungo Park by the king of Dahomey—'What do they think of us in England?' This being the case, as it is, though it may be indignantly denied, how great is the responsibility of the English people, in the matter of American slavery! It is not too much to affirm, that it lies in their hands. The dominion of the slave power is so fastened upon us by the weak and wicked compact which our fathers made with it, that there is no political machinery that can be put in operation for its overthrow; because, by that compact, the control of the whole political machinery is put into its hands.

"No aristocracy ever yet resigned its power, except upon compulsion. The only compulsion in this case is that of the public opinion of the world—AND ENGLAND IS THE WORLD TO AMERICA.

"Let the general mind of England (using that term for the empire,) become thoroughly possessed of the facts of American slavery, and obey the impulses which such facts must create in every generous bosom, and the hand of destiny will have written the words of doom upon the walls of our Babylon."

ed many years in the countries where the principal scenes of this narrative have been enacted, he may, without presumption, lay claim to a right of judgment as to the probability of Benjamin Benson's adventures. After a careful investigation of all the attendant circumstances in connection with his statements, the writer pronounces this to be, in his opinion, A TALE OF TRUTH, and one which cannot fail to interest all who possess the feelings of men and christians—more particularly in regard to such as profess an abhorrence of slavery.

A NARRATIVE
OF THE LIFE OF
BENJAMIN BENSON.

THE father of Benjamin Benson was a native of Gambia, in Africa, and was taken away from his country, when a child, in a slave ship, to the West Indies—to what island is not known; but he was brought, as a slave, to Bermuda, some years before the birth of the subject of this narrative. His mother was born a slave upon Long Island, New York; and, at the age of twelve years, was sold to a Mr. Davenport, in Bermuda, where the parents of Benson were united, but whether by lawful marriage or otherwise is not known.

They had twenty-one children; among the number were twins. One or two died when young, the remainder lived to be men and women. Although the parents dwelt together long enough to have so large a family, they were at length separated by the cruel laws of slavery, when Benjamin was but eight years of age. His father and his brother George, with a sister named Judith, were taken to Georgia, in the United States. Another sister, Sally, was purchased free by a Quaker named Stephen Craft, and taken by him to New York, where she lived in his family as a servant, and was treated with much kindness. She remained with these good people until she married a man of her own colour, named John Williams, a native of New York, by whom she had six children. She died in 1843, and her children are still living with their father in their native town.

One brother, Robert, was sold in Bermuda, and taken to Wilmington, North Carolina, from whence, under favour of a merciful Providence, he made his escape to New York, to which town he was pursued by the human bloodhounds of the south. Fearing he might be apprehended, and again consigned to the horrors of slavery, when he would be sure to receive the torture that awaits a refugee, he changed his name to Tripp, and took passage, as an emigrant, to Trinidad, where he still resides in happy security.

A brother, named Anthony, was the property of Miss Davenport, in Bermuda. This young lady died at the age of eighteen, bequeathing to Anthony his freedom. He was some months employed in a pilot-boat, until a Wesleyan Missionary, named Smith, came to the Island and invited this brother to accompany him to New York, and there procured for him a situation in a tea warehouse, with a gentleman who took much pains to improve his education, and to direct his mind towards Heaven. Anthony is now studying with a view to become a preacher of the Gospel of Christ.

The following well written letter was received by Benjamin Benson, in England, in the month of April, 1846:—

"New-York, March 24th, 1846.
"MY DEAR BROTHER,
"Your letter of the 4th November has been received,

and it has afforded me great pleasure in hearing from you, who have been so long far away from us. I have a good prospect before me—better, I think, than I ever had before. I am in the employment of the same house still, and have been for two years, and am at present studying for the Ministry.

"I devote from eight o'clock till eleven, p.m. in preparing myself, until the 1st of May, and at that time a company of gentlemen intend to give me the means to support me at the University for three years, in order that my mind may be qualified for the work. I desire in this life, as far as lies in me, to be useful or instrumental in saving souls from eternal ruin ; and, my dear brother, if we never meet again this side of *Canaan's happy shore*, I pray that we both may meet in heaven, to praise Him who has suffered, bled, and died for lost and undone sinners, as we are, '*where the wicked cease from troubling, and the weary are at rest.*'

"I have to communicate to you, in this letter, the death of our dear sister Sally, who departed this life about three years ago, of a fever. '*Blessed are the dead that die in the Lord.*' Brother John * is well, and joins in sending his love to you. He is doing well for this life, as far as worldly matters are concerned ; but I hope that he may be brought to see this world as nothing, and to seek the path which leads to God.

"It may be, in the providence of God, that we may meet again on this earth, but if not, the Lord's will be done. I am a temperate man, and go for teetotalism, and hope you may be temperate in all things. I lecture upon that subject.

"When you write to me, please address 'Anthony Benson, Zion's Church, corner of Church and Leonard-street, New York.' I here close.

"And remain,
"Your affectionate brother,
"ANTHONY BENSON."

* The husband of Sally.

The other branches of the Benson family were sold before the birth of Benjamin, and he does not know in what part of the world they are, or if they are yet living.

Benjamin Benson was born December 16th, 1818, at St. George's, in the Island of Bermuda, and inhaled the first breath of life as a slave. His early days were spent in the capacity of house boy, which situation is far preferable to that of a common labourer or field hand, as that class of slaves are denominated. When about eight years old, he was cut with a knife over the left eye, as a private mark of his mistress, by which he could at any time be known in case he should be stolen, or if he should attempt to seek his liberty. This mark not being considered sufficient by his master, he caused him to be branded with a red hot iron upon his right shoulder, both which marks are very distinct at the present moment.*

---

* The cruel infliction of marks upon the persons of the negroes is common throughout slaveholding countries. It is not unusual for them to be branded with the initials of their owners, with red-hot irons, upon the back, breast, and inner part of the thighs. Sometimes the top or bottom of the ear is cut off, and not unfrequently one ear entirely severed.—ED.

The following advertisements will furnish specimens of the cruelties committed, and of the indifference with which the social condition of the slaves—their ties of kindred and affections, are regarded by the white inhabitants of the Southern States :—

"TWENTY DOLLARS REWARD.—Ran away from the subscriber, a negro girl, named Molly. She is sixteen or seventeen years of age, slim made, lately *branded on the left cheek, thus—'R,'* and a *piece taken off her ear* on the same side ; *the same letter on the inside of both her legs.*

"ABNER Ross, Fairfield District."

From the Charleston Courier.

Although his days, up to twelve years old, were spent in comparative comfort, still the joys of freedom were denied him; he often suffered severe punishment for slight offences, and freqently for none. He was sometimes whipped because his master's child cried, and remembers being severely flogged because the dog barked. At length he was sold to an American named Sneed, and by him taken to Mobile. The following sentiments do honor to his mind:—" I had often reflected," said Benson, "upon my former condition, and fancied that my lot in life could not be more wretched, and for a moment I felt an inward joy at the prospect of a change; but when I took leave of my mother, who was very fond of me, and parted with the companions of my childhood, I felt desolate and wept, and as soon as I had left my native land I felt the full force of my forlorn condition. As the ship gradually left but a dim speck of the island, my heart almost burst with grief, and I again

"One Hundred Dollars will be given for my two *fellows*. Abram and Frank. Abram has a *wife* at Col. Stewart's, in *Liberty(?)* County, and a *sister* in Savannah, at Captain Govensting's. Frank has a *wife* at Mr. Le Cont's, in *Liberty(?)* County, a *mother* at Thunderbolt, and a *sister* in Savannah.
"Wm. Roberts."
From the Savannah Georgian.

"Fifty Dollars Reward.—Ran away, Paulidore, commonly called Paul. I understand Gen. R. Y. Hayne has purchased his *wife* and *children*, and has them now on his plantation, at Goosecreek, where, no doubt, the *fellow* is frequently *lurking*.
Ibid. "T. Davis."

"Ran Away—A negro woman and two children. A few days before she went off, *I burned her with a hot iron* on the left side of her face. I *tried* to make the letter M.
"Micajah Ricks."
From the Raleigh Standard

gave vent to my sorrow in tears, when, instead of comfort and consolation, I received cuffs and kicks as a 'snivelling scoundrel.'"

As the evening closed in, young Benson, with the rest of the human cargo, consisting of about 300 slaves, were ordered to go down below, where they were placed in rows, and, thus seated, the legs of one portion passed between the ones of those who sat opposite to them; by which contrivance they occupied as small a space as possible. In this uneasy position they were fed upon Indian meal and coarse grease from long troughs, twice a day. These troughs were similar to those commonly used for hogs, which extended along the whole line of the miserable sufferers. The ones who ate the fastest of course were best fed. Several pined away by grief and want of proper nourishment, and as soon as they were freed from their wretchedness by the hand of death, they became food for numerous sharks that followed the vessel. In this manner they passed fourteen days, until the ship reached Mobile.

Benson had heard much of cruelty used by Americans towards their slaves, and he now gazed upon the dreary shore with feelings of despair. His mother had early taught him to look to the Lord, and he lifted up his voice in prayer, and received comfort; but his applications for help from Heaven were, of necessity, made in secret from all but "*Him from whom no secrets are hid.*" Several of his fellow captives were detected in the act of imploring mercy from the Saviour, when they were immediately scourged by a whip made of raw cow-hide. Well might they have exclaimed, "*Oh! ye tyrants! we call Heaven and earth to record this day against you.*"

On landing at Mobile, they were marched in pairs, fastened together by the wrists, to the "house of health," where they met many more wretched sufferers, some of whom had been smuggled in from Africa. After having undergone examination by the "health officer," to discover if any disease existed among them, they were conducted to the yards of the different persons to whom they were sold.

On the following morning Benson was put to work in the cotton fields, and remained thus occupied for a fortnight, during which time he was treated with no great degree of severity. His owner, it is supposed, considered temporary indulgence necessary to recruit the weakened frame of his new purchase, who had suffered much through grief and privation on the passage.

He was now removed to a rice plantation belonging to his owner, near New Orleans. Here he soon began to experience the bitterness of American slavery. His labour lasted from the rising to the setting of the sun. The slaves were allowed but half-an-hour to breakfast, an hour to dinner, and an hour after work, to wash and refresh themselves; when they were locked up in a yard, in the centre of which was a fire that served for warmth and to cook their food; which, with the rest of their meals, consisted of parched Indian corn and what opossums and other wild animals of the same character they occasionally caught in traps during their dinner hours. Around the yard were a few miserable huts for them to sleep in, until they were aroused from their slumbers by the loud crack of the driver's whip, to resume their daily toil in swampy land, frequently up to their knees in mud and water for weeks together. In this occupation the mosquitoes and sand-flies were very tormenting. Many of the slaves also suffered much from the bites of water-scorpions and other noxious reptiles.

This kind of labour was very severe to one who had not been accustomed to the constant stooping posture it required. Poor Benson would sometimes attempt to relieve himself by erecting his body, when he was speedily reminded by a stroke of the driver's long whip that such an indulgence was not permitted. And when, from excessive fatigue, he slackened in his labour, he would be taken to a whipping-post, to receive twenty-five or thirty lashes upon the bare skin. Even speaking to a fellow slave, was often considered an offence sufficient to incur such a torture.

Whipping-posts are placed in different parts of the plantation, some of which are made single, with iron shackles to receive the wrists and ankles; others are formed of two posts, with a cross-beam at the top, about eight feet high, to which the arms are suspended by cords made fast to the wrists, and drawn up by pulleys; the feet are confined by iron shackles affixed to a log of wood. In this posture, sufficiently painful in itself, Benson often received the scourge of the whip until the blood ran in streams down his legs. "*Often,*" says he, "*have I inwardly prayed to the Lord that he would end my sufferings by death;*" and sometimes he felt tempted to put an end to his miserable existence by self-destruction, " but," he continues, "*as I had at all times been relieved by prayer, I trusted to the Lord for his mercy.*"*

For two years he endured this life of toil and wretchedness. At length he was sold to a man named Tech, and removed to Washington, in North Carolina. Although no longer compelled to work in swamps, with all the annoyances spoken of; still his labour appears to have been rather increased than mitigated, being now obliged to work in a turpentine factory from daylight till eight o'clock at night, and oftentimes a great portion of the night; also, his punishments were about as usual. Never was he looked upon as a human being, much less as a christian. Such was the desire to keep the slaves in ignorance, that upon one occasion one of his fellows in

---

* I have known a negro punished in the following manner:—He was laid upon the ground, with his arms and legs extended, which were secured to the earth by wooden pegs, to which his wrists and ankles were fastened by rope-yarns. Fifty lashes were then applied to the bare skin of the posteriors, every one of which took out a piece of flesh. To increase the torture, in this instance, the wretched man was laid on an *ant-heap*, and before the flogging had ceased, myriads of these venomous insects covered his body—thus was he left for an hour to endure torments worse than a hundred deaths.—Ed.

bondage received twenty-five lashes for presuming to say he had *a soul to be saved!*

Mr. Tech took much delight in having a certain number of his slaves trained as prize-fighters, who were regularly pitted against some of those of his neighbours, by which laudable amusement he sometimes won, but more frequently lost large sums of money. Four or five of the handsomest and most robust were kept in luxurious ease and idleness, well clad and well fed, to be let out occasionally for purposes that must be unexplained; it is sufficient to state that they were fathers to some hundreds of slave children.*

In consequence of the gambling propensities of Mr. Tech, with his prize-fighting slaves, cock-fighting, dog-fighting, bull-fighting, and other equally humane pursuits, aided by hard drinking, he soon became so involved in difficulties as to have his slaves

---

* It is well known that in the slave-breeding States, the negroes are bred and reared precisely as cattle; and at the age of eight or ten years are taken from their parents and sent to the more southern states, to be sold to the cotton and sugar plantations.

"But the climax of infamy is still untold. This trade in blood—this buying, imprisoning, and exporting of boys and girls—this tearing asunder of husbands and wives, parents and children; it is all legalized *in virtue of authority delegated by Congress.* The 249th page of the laws of THE CITY OF WASHINGTON, dated 28th July, 1838, contains the following enactment:—FOR A LICENCE TO TRADE OR TRAFFIC IN SLAVES, FOR PROFIT, FOUR HUNDRED DOLLARS!!!

"It is calculated that not less than 80,000 slaves are sent away every year from the slave-breeding to the slave-*consuming* States."— *Slavery and the Slave Trade, by Robert Kaye Greville, L.L.D.*

Women, as early after confinement as possible, sometimes but a few days, are sent to the field to work, while the infants are placed together in pens, their mothers being sent to them occasionally to suckle them, in the same manner as cows are driven home to their calves.—ED.

brought to the hammer at public auction, when Benjamin Benson was once more sold. On the morning of the sale, a number, amounting to several hundreds of men, women, and children, were brought to market, this being market day. They were placed alternately, when not sold in lots, upon a molasses cask or a rum puncheon in a state of nudity, when they were scrutinized with the same caution that a jockey displays in purchasing a horse. One examined Benson's limbs, and caused him to jump about, and by way of assisting him in this involuntary performance, he every now and then had applied to him a smart cut of a whip. He was made to throw his arms and legs about in every direction to see that his limbs were perfect. Another made him open his mouth to discover whether his teeth were in good order, and gave him hard biscuits to test the strength of his grinders. In fact every expedient was resorted to by a purchaser to detect a flaw, and every species of jockeyship that is usually had rescourse to in selling a horse, was exercised by the ingenious vendue-master to set off each slave to the best advantage.

As the negroes were knocked down to the highest bidder, many, Benson among the number, were marched to the shipping yard, manacled in pairs, in the same manner as that in which they were landed at Mobile.

"I can hardly attempt," says Benjamin Benson, "to describe the scene of distress upon this occasion.

As fathers took a last farewell of their wives and children, or children of their parents, brothers or sisters, a general shriek of agony burst from us all as we turned our streaming eyes towards our relations, or friends who had become endeared to each other as fellows in bondage. Our distress was met by jeers and coarse jokes; and at times by the most impious curses of our white oppressors, many of whom applied the lash to our backs for thus giving vent to our sorrows. Even at the present hour," continues Benson, " I look back to that event with feelings of deepest horror, and often have I found my face wet with tears on awaking from a dream, when the whole scene has been brought fresh before me."*

He now became the property of Thomas Trot, who took him to St. Christophers, in the West Indies. The treatment of the slaves on this passage was much the same as that from Bermuda to America, excepting that, as the vessel was larger, they were permitted to be more frequently on deck, and they were not so much incommoded for room when below. On arriv-

---

* It is seldom one can take up a newspaper in the southern States without noticing such advertisements as the following :—

" ONE HUNDRED AND TWENTY NEGROES FOR SALE.—The subscriber has just arrived from Petersburgh, Virginia, with one hundred and twenty *likely young negroes, of both sexes*, and of every description, which he offers for sale on most reasonable terms." In the *lot* are described " several women with children, *small girls, suitable for nurses,* and *several small boys*, WITHOUT THEIR MOTHERS.—Benjamin Davis." *Charleston Papers.*

Slaves are driven from Virginia, and other slave breeding districts, in gangs of from 50 to 500, called *cobbles*, fastened together by handcuffs and chains, to be sold to the " slave consuming States."—ED.

ing at St. Christophers or St. Kitts, as it is usually called, some of the slaves were landed for plantations there, the remainder, Benson among the number, proceeded in the same ship to Bermuda, where he had the satisfaction of once more beholding his much loved mother. She had sadly changed since he left her—grief at the loss of her husband and children had rendered her feeble and careworn, so that she appeared to be many years older than she really was Her son's person was also much changed since they parted, he having now become a man; so much in fact was he altered, that his mother could not have recognized him but for the marks that had been cut and branded upon his skin. He was now indulged with three days to himself, which were the first holidays he had ever known. Most of this time he spent with his mother, or as much of it as when she could be spared from her work, she being at the same time herself a slave.

Benson was delighted to find the condition of the slaves in his native country much improved by late orders from the English Government. All were anxiously looking forward to the glorious and joyful time when they would be FREE, and placed upon an equal footing with the rest of the children of God. Emancipation had been already promised them, and the dark cloud of tyranny was gradually lifting from the horizon. A bow of hope was already visible in the heavens. With hearts full of gratitude did they fervently, and now unrestrained and unmolested, offer up their prayers and petitions to the Blessed Saviour, that he would speedily redeem them from bondage. The Lord heard their supplications. From this time the shriek of agony caused by the lash seldom met the ear. They were treated with a kindness that seemed a harbinger of their fondest hope—FREEDOM.

The life of Benson passed on tranquilly and cheerfully until the glorious Jubilee of Liberty arrived, when not a foot of ground throughout the British dominions could be trodden by a slave, and each negro, from the lisping babe to tottering old age, in the fulness of his joy exclaimed—I AM A MAN—I AM FREE!!!

None but those who have passed their days in slavery, when every action, every will, every word, and almost every thought is at the disposal of another, can appreciate the blessing of liberty.

Benjamin now luxuriated in the full enjoyment of freedom, and for the first time felt that he ranked among human beings. His thanks were offered up night and morning to the great God of mercy for his goodness. And it was pleasing to hear thousands, who but a short time since pined in bondage, now freely singing, with joyous hearts, in all the fulness of gratitude, their praises to the Lord.

We are too apt to forget the extent of Divine grace, and to think ourselves secured from future harm when we have been suddenly lifted up by prosperity. Alas! how frail—how futile are all human dependencies. The cup of Benson's misery remained yet to be filled. It had been taken from his lips for a moment to be replaced by the sweets of happiness, but for one brief moment only, as will be proved in the course of the narrative.

He continued upon his native island about a year, when he was induced to trust himself once more upon the deep, and he embarked on board the *Egbert*, Captain Norie, and sailed for New York, where he had the good fortune to meet his brother Anthony. From thence he went to Halifax and back to Bermuda, nothing remarkable having occurred during this voyage.

His aged mother depended in a great measure upon her son Benjamin for support, and as he could earn more money by going to sea, he once more left Bermuda in the schooner *Jane*, and sailed again for New York. In this thriving city there are many who are friendly to the abolition of slavery, and who do not disdain to treat a coloured man with kindness and respect; but the generality of white inhabitants there look upon the negro race as beings of an inferior order, so that Benson was often exposed to annoyances and insults when on shore, but being of a quiet disposition, he seldom allowed himself to resent any act of oppression. The following ludicrous scene appears to have afforded him no little amusement as well as gratification:—During his stay in the port of New York, he observed a coloured man walking quietly down the street with his comrades, who were

British sailors belonging to an English ship, when they were met by a gentleman and lady. As the coloured man did not immediately make room at their approach upon the side walk, the gentleman (?) used abusive language, which was patiently borne by the black, until the white man seized him by the collar of his jacket, when the coloured man laid hold upon his antagonist in a similar manner.

The gentleman now let go his grip and entered a shop, where he bought a cow-hide whip, which being observed by one of the sailors, he instantly bounded to the same place and made a similar purchase, which he placed in the hand of his black friend. As soon as the gentleman commenced operations, he was astonished to find that every cut of his whip was returned with painful interest, amidst the loud cheers of the sailors, and the bitter curses of many Americans, who were shocked to see a white man flogged by a *nigger*. At the same time they considered it safest not to interfere with British tars. It was not long before the gentleman had received more than what he conceived consistent with his dignity, and was fain to make a hasty retreat.

No one who has not resided in the United States can form an idea as to the distance that exists between the white and the coloured people. The prejudice is not confined to the slave districts, where such a barrier existing does not excite much astonishment; but in the northern States also, where it was only reasonable to expect that when they had cast off the odious stigma of slavery, the film would have fallen from their eyes, and they would have viewed all men born in the country as equal; and with such high pretensions to christianity, it might have been expected that there would have existed a pervading feeling of brotherly love.*

Benson left the schooner *Jane* in New York, and sailed in several small coasting vessels for about a year. He at length shipped on board the American ship *William Goddard*, captain Potter, and sailed from New York to Mobile, where he remained seven weeks. As he was a coloured man he was not allowed to set his foot on shore once during the whole time.

The *William Goddard* afterwards called at Saint Mark's and Appalachicola, in Florida, to complete the cargo of cotton. During his stay at the latter port he learned that his father and a brother were slaves upon Mr. Milner's plantation near the town, but he was not allowed to see either of them, nor even to hold conversation with any coloured man who came on board, as soon as it was known that he had relations there in slavery. All he could find out was that his father was very old and very cruelly used. Not being able to do much work, he was supported

* Such is the distance at which the coloured people are held by the strong arm of prejudice in America, that however distinguished a man may be by wealth, education, virtue, or piety—who, in fact, may lay every claim to the character of a gentleman—if it be known that he has a drop of African blood in his veins, he is excluded from the society and privileges of white people. In hotels, steam-boats, stage coaches, theatres, churches, and even in burying grounds he is compelled to take a different station.—ED.

chiefly by the charity of his fellow-slaves, his brother having but little opportunity of assisting him. Benjamin was much distressed by this intelligence. He would gladly have sent a portion of his wages to his poor old father, but he was so closely watched as to render such an act of filial duty impossible, and no coloured man dared undertake to open a correspondence between them.

He now sailed for Liverpool, in England*—in truth

* To show how impartially justice is here administered to all without distinction of colour or country, and how powerful is the bulwark of British freedom, where not only are all classes shielded from oppression, but the breath of slander is instantly strangled, the following interesting correspondence is inserted. The Rev. Dr. Smyth is heartily congratulated upon the ridiculous position in which he has placed himself, and the condolence he must necessarily have received from his fellow slave-owners on his return to Charlestown, for having apologised so abjectly to a *Nigger* :—

FROM THE " NORTHERN WHIG," 8TH AUG. 1846.
" *Mr. Frederick Douglass and Rev. Doctor Smyth.*
" TO THE EDITOR OF THE ' NORTHERN WHIG.'

" Sir,—The Rev. Doctor Thomas Smyth, of Charlestown, South Carolina, who lately visited Belfast, made certain statements injurious to the moral and religious character of Mr. Frederick Douglass, the fugitive slave.

" These statements being calculated to injure his usefulness, Mr. Douglass felt himself compelled, for the sake of his brethren in bonds, and in justice to the Belfast Anti-slavery Society, who invited him to this town, and especially to prevent others from defending slavery, or shielding its abettors, by calumniating him, to call upon the Rev. gentleman to come forward and make a full and public apology, or abide the legal consequences of refusal. Messrs. Davison and Torrens, solicitors, on behalf of Mr. Douglass, demanded this apology from Dr. Smyth, intimating at the same time, that, in case of refusal, he must abide the issue of a civil action, which would afford him abundant opportunity to prove (if he could) the truth of his assertions. Mr. Douglass, conscious of innocence, took this manly and fearless mode of procedure, rather than the more usual one of filing a criminal information, which would hinder the party complained against from putting in a plea of justification.

" I have the pleasure of handing you, by desire of Mr. Douglass, "the land of the brave and the free"—and returned in the same ship to New Orleans. On the passage thither he was very cruelly treated, both by the captain and chief mate, who frequently beat him severely with handspikes and belaying-pins. His shipmates were very kind to him, and pitied his miserable condition, but dared not interfere. Such continued oppression to one who now laid claim to all the rights and privileges of a free man, became at length beyond endurance, and in a moment of excitement he attempted resistance, which only brought upon him an increase of cruelty.*

(who is now in England) a copy of Doctor Smyth's letter of apology, with which Mr. Douglass's solicitors advised him to rest satisfied, as his only object was the vindication of principle and character, and not any consideration of a pecuniary nature.

"This transaction, Sir, is a noble illustration of the spirit of British law, which, as Curran said, makes justice commensurate with, and inseparable from British soil; which proclaims even to the stranger, the moment he sets his foot on our shore, that the ground is consecrated by the genius of universal emancipation.

"I am, your obedient servant,
"JAMES STANDFIELD."
"Belfast, 7th Aug. 1846."
(COPY.)
"'Dublin, July 28th, 1846.

"'GENTLEMEN,—In reply to your letter of the 16th instant, informing me that you had been instructed by Mr. Frederick Douglass, the anti-slavery lecturer, to institute proceedings at law against me for certain statements made by me injurious to his moral and religious character, I beg to express my sincere regret for having uttered the same; the more especially as, upon mature reflection, I am quite satisfied that the statements I incautiously made, on the report of third parties, were unfounded.

"'Very respectfully,
"'Your obedient servant,
"'THOMAS SMYTH.'"

"'Messrs. Davison and Torrens.'"

* Black men generally engage themselves as stewards and cooks in ships, and I have often been witness to the oppression and cruelty exercised towards them by the captains and mates.—ED.

When the ship arrived at Belise, the entrance of the Mississippi river, Benson was reported to the officer in command of the custom-house boat, as having been guilty of mutiny. Consequently he was handcuffed and taken to the calaboose or prison, at New Orleans, where, without the formality of a trial, he was severely flogged, and placed with other criminals into the chain-gang. The chain-gangs are chiefly composed of slaves who have attempted to make their escape. They are in parties of from twenty to fifty. Each individual has his ankle chained by an iron ring to his fellow-prisoner, to which chain is not unfrequently affixed an iron weight of from fourteen to twenty-five pounds, and in this manner they are driven with long whips, with far less mercy than would be extended towards any of the brute portion of creation.*

In this deplorable condition Benson continued for nine weeks,† at the expiration of which time he was sold to pay the jail expenses, and sent to a plantation belonging to a Mr. Woodfork, where he continued

---

* When any ladies or gentlemen in New Orleans do not think fit to punish their slaves themselves, or to have them flogged at home, they have only to send them to the jail with a dollar, and an order, specifying the number of lashes required to be inflicted, which mandate is invariably complied with, without the least enquiry as to the offence.—ED.

† The laws of Florida, Alabama, Georgia, Louisiana, Mississippi, and South Carolina are, that any coloured person coming by sea, the steward, captain, or owner of the vessel, in any of the ports must be imprisoned, and the vessel charged with the costs; and should he not depart in due time, all the fees and costs having been first paid for his imprisonment, he is to be sold as a slave for ninety-nine years, and the proceeds are put into the county treasury.—ED.

working in the cotton fields for a year, when he effected his escape in the night, in which he was assisted by a young English gentleman, who conducted him to the river side, and pointed out the light of a steam-boat in the stream, about half-a-mile distant. He desired him to wait on the shore until he heard the town clock strike twelve, telling him by that time he would be on board the steam-boat to receive him.

Benson passed an hour and a half in painful anxiety, fearing he might be missed from the plantation, and search made for him. The night was dark, and the stillness only broken by the terrific roar of the alligators, or when one plunged from the bank into the river.* At times his courage failed him, under apprehension that he might become a prey to these monsters; but when he reflected upon the certainty of punishment, little short of death, that awaited him, should he be taken as a runaway, he preferred to risk the danger of being devoured.† He had already known the joys of freedom, and anticipated the delight of again beholding his beloved mother.

* Alligators are very large and numerous in the south. The writer shot one which measured fifteen feet, and they have been killed measuring twenty feet.

† It appears Terry (the owner of two slaves who escaped from Covington, Louisiana,) had tobacco hogsheads filled with wrought nails, driven in from the outside, so that they projected inside the hogshead. The wretched slave was then placed in, *and the head fastened on.* In this place of torment they were rolled round the slave quarters, to strike terror into the slaves. On every turn *the nails were driven into the flesh, till they were literally bleeding at every pore.* When taken out, they were rubbed down with *brine and pepper,* and then washed with *rum.—Speech of Mr. Johnson, at the World's Convention.*

At length the solemn hour of midnight struck upon his ear, and after offering up a prayer to the Father of Mercies, he quietly let himself into the water, and boldly struck out. He had not proceeded far when another formidable difficulty presented itself. He discovered that, in consequence of heavy rains having recently fallen in the interior of the country, the current was much more rapid than usual, consequently he deemed it expedient to return to the shore, and take a fresh departure nearly a mile higher up, that he might not be carried by the force of the stream below the object of his hope.

Again he consigned himself to the care of the Almighty, and cautiously (but not without increased dread of the alligators, which were now roaring around him in great numbers) slid quietly into the turbid water. Being an expert swimmer, he apprehended little difficulty from the distance, but dreaded he might miss the vessel, as he was now considerably beyond sight of it. Fortunately, as soon as he had reached near the centre of the river, he discerned the steam-boat below him. Allowing himself to drift under the bow, he seized a rope, by which he sustained himself until his kind friend and preserver, Mr. S——, who was anxiously watching for his arrival, heard his low whistle, (the preconcerted signal.) With the assistance of the second mate, who was made privy to the plan of Benson's escape, he was taken on board, and secretly conveyed below, where he remained until the vessel reached Nassau, in New

Providence, when he made his appearance upon deck, to the astonishment of the captain, who either was, or pretended to be, very angry at the discovery; but as it was a vessel in an English port, Benson, without entering into any explanation, deliberately betook himself to the shore. He sought an early opportunity of throwing himself at the feet of his preserver, and thanking him with unfeigned gratitude.

For the first few days after his liberation, he almost lost his senses in the extacy of his joy: he wept and laughed every hour in the day, throwing himself upon his knees in humble thanksgiving to the Saviour of all. He could neither eat nor sleep for three successive days and nights; and he feels assured, were it not for the soothing effect of prayer, that he must have exchanged the chains of slavery for those of a lunatic.

As Mr. S. had frequent intercourse with New Orleans, and as the steam-boat in which Benjamin Benson made his escape, often called at that port, it must be obvious to the reader that it would be improper to introduce the names of either the passenger or the Captain.*

* This benevolent gentleman ran no little risk of being hanged for his humane exertions in aiding the escape of a slave, as the following examples will testify :

A young man named Brown was under sentence of death for aiding a young woman to make her escape from South Carolina, and it was only at the intercession of the English Government, that his sentence was commuted to imprisonment for life.

The Rev. Charles T. Torry died in prison, at Baltimore, on the 9th of May, 1846. He had been incarcerated for attempting to rescue his fellow-christians from slavery.

"No man can give a piece of bread to a poor man, if he happens

It cannot have escaped observation, that hitherto the names of persons and places have been given without a single reservation.

After remaining a week at Nassau, he embarked in a schooner for Bermuda, where he arrived once more in safety, and had the pleasure to find his mother in good health, although she had suffered much anxiety in not having heard from Benjamin for such a length of time.

During his bondage at Woodfork's plantation, a circumstance happened of so remarkable a character, that the writer of this narrative cannot forego the opportunity of placing it before the public. It is one which clearly demonstrates that the Almighty does not always delay his judgment until the measure of sin be fulfilled. The ready chastisement of an offended God, in the present instance, ought to have filled the mind of every slave-holder with dread, and at the same time to have convinced him that the Lord will protect the innocent, and not fail to punish the guilty.

An English missionary* came to the plantation,

to be a slave; no man can receive him to his house, and harbour him for the night, to preserve him from his pursuer, without subjecting himself to a penalty of 500 dollars, and imprisonment for six months."
—*From a speech of the Rev. H. H. Kellog, at the World's Convention.*

* It would be unjust to state that there are no truly christian ministers of the gospel of Christ in the slave states of America; but such as there are, are so restricted by the laws and prejudices of the slave-holders, as to find it impossible to impart religious instruction to the slaves, without in some measure leaning towards their "*peculiar* institution." Such men may be pitied rather than condemned; but when clergymen, "Heaven's heralds," unblushingly become the advocates of slavery—not only the advocates, but absolutely owners

with a letter of introduction to Mr. Woodfork, from whom he requested permission for his slaves to attend at a prayer-meeting. In compliment to his friend, from whom the missionary had come recommended, the request was granted, at the same time under a promise that slavery should not in any way be reverted to, and that the negroes should be back to the yard by ten o'clock at night.

At this meeting a young mulatto woman named Margaret, a house servant, generally supposed to be the child of her master, who had been up to the pre-

and dealers in the persons of their fellow-creatures—the heart of the philanthropist burns with indignation. That there are many such hypocrites can be easily demonstrated.

The Rev. Dr. Gadsden, Episcopal vicar at Charlestown, South Carolina, owned many slaves, and hired out a portion of them for the purpose of erecting a new church. The screams of those poor wretches might be heard daily, as they writhed beneath the torturing lash of the driver, within the walls of the sanctuary to be dedicated to the Father of Mercy.

The Rev. Mr. Smith, a Presbyterian minister of Livingston, Sumpter county, Alabama, owned twenty slaves.

The Rev. Mr. M'Donald, Presbyterian minister, married a lady in Florida, as he acknowledged, for the purpose of being the owner of many slaves, whom he subsequently treated with much severity.

The Methodist Episcopal Bishop, Andrews, was superseded for being a slave-holder.

It is a well known fact, that the Synod of South Carolina and Georgia, *sold eight of their fellow creatures, for the purpose of educating Presbyterian ministers!!! O tempore! O mores!*

The clergy in the slave states stand even prior to the parent, in influencing the minds, and in directing the conduct of youth. The slave-owner, from earliest childhood, is taught to revere the opinions of ministers of religion as above those of all others, and when they themselves become, not only advocates of slavery, but who also become dealers in human beings, and proprietors of their persons, can we be surprised that laymen should continue in ignorance of what is right upon this vital question, and persevere in the maintenance of erroneous opinions. Take away the clerical supports, and the whole rotten fabric will fall to the ground.—Ed.

sent moment, as were most of the slaves throughout the state of Louisiana, a Roman Catholic, but through the persuasion of the missionary at the meeting, she became suddenly a convert to the Baptist church. The poor girl, in her devotion to the Lord Jesus, overstayed her limited time by a few minutes. On her return to the dwelling-house of her owners, she was met by her mistress, Mrs. Woodfork, to whom she exclaimed, in the fulness of her heart, "Oh! mistress, I have joyful news to tell"—and was proceeding with a detail of her conversion, in which she was suddenly arrested by her mistress telling her that she had better not let her hear any more of her nonsense, and immediately took her into the back kitchen, and flogged her severely for overstaying her time.

A short while after she had received this cruel and unmerited chastisement, the son, George Woodfork, (who, if the former statement be correct, was Margaret's brother) came home, and seeing the poor girl still weeping, with sobs of deep affliction, he enquired of his mother the cause. No sooner had he been informed that she had overstayed her time at the prayer-meeting, for which she had just been punished, than, seizing the cow-hide whip, which his mother still retained in her hand, "She is laughing at you," said he; "you have not given her half enough"—and calling upon God to eternally damn him, (his usual expression of blasphemy) if he did not put a stop to her snivelling. He raised his arm to inflict more torture upon the wretched girl, with another bitter curse upon his lip, when the arm fell powerless by his side.—HE WAS SEIZED WITH A PARALYTIC STROKE.

Benson staid six months with his mother in Bermuda, occupying his time in working on board different vessels, but finding he could not earn so much money in this way as by long voyages, he again bade adieu to his mother, and sailed in the brig *Pamplico*, for Washington, North Carolina. During his stay in this port he was permitted to go on shore. Upon one occasion he was rudely thrust off the side-walk by a white man, who told him that was no place for *niggers*. Benson very naturally expostulated upon this act of injustice, when he received a violent blow. To save himself from further injury, he laid hold of the white man by the collar. Constables were called, and Benson was taken before a magistrate, who ordered two of his fingers to be put into an iron screw, purposely constructed as a torture for coloured offenders, by which he had the top of one squeezed off to the first joint, and the other was much injured. When the magistrate passed this inhuman sentence upon Benson, he informed him that had he struck his white antagonist, he should have ordered his arm to be cut off, if he did not even pass sentence of death upon him.* In addition to this

* After a residence of nearly a quarter of a century in slave-holding countries, I could adduce a thousand instances of cruelty and oppression towards the slaves, that would be too horrible for recital. I have known a father, in a drunken freak, level his rifle at his own mulatto

decree, Benson was ordered to pay ten dollars for Court expences. As he had not so much yet due him from his ship, he had a narrow escape of being again sold as a slave, and it was only at the kind interference of the English Consul that he was spared from such a doom.

He returned in the *Pamplico* to Bermuda, and went to live with a Mr. Martin, an arrow-root merchant, who treated him with much kindness. With this gentleman he came to England, and spent some weeks in Cheltenham. His master took him back

child in the cradle, and shoot it dead. I have known several poor wretched negroes die from the lash, and have seen an aged negro trampled to death beneath the horse's feet of its rider. But all that I have seen—all that I have heard of, is nothing to be compared to the diabolical act of LEGAL human slaughter that took place in New Orleans, April 21st, 1845—the execution of the girl Pauline for *striking* her mistress.

The melancholy tale must be in the remembrance of some of my readers.

Pauline was in the full bloom of health and beauty, not more than nineteen years of age. She was so nearly white that, in this country, no difference in colour would have been observed.

It appears her charms had attracted the lustful desires of her master, to whose absolute dominion she was compelled to yield, and became in a fair way to add another to his stock of human chattels. The circumstance naturally excited the jealousy of his wife, who continually, with the savage vengeance of a she-wolf, goaded Pauline with the lash, until, in a moment of excitement, she gave her mistress a a blow—A SINGLE BLOW, for the hundreds she had received. It was enough—she was instantly thrown into prison to await her trial. She was tried, found guilty, and condemned to be hanged, for having done that which might have been committed with impunity by any white man, woman, or child, throughout the United States, upon the whole number of three millions of slaves in the south.

The murder of Pauline was delayed until she gave birth to a female child—to become, in all probability, another victim to some monster of humanity. The execution took place in the public streets, where elegant carriages filled with *ladies(?)* were ranged up amidst the throng of thousands who hailed the wretched and unpitied girl with exclamations of brutal satisfaction when she came upon the scaffold.

with him to Bermuda, when he had the happiness to find his mother in comfortable circumstances, he having made over to her half his pay.

Benson continued in the service of Mr. Martin, and made another trip with him to England. He spent five weeks of his stay in Brighton, and subsequently accompanied his master to New York, and from thence back to Bermuda, where he remained during the winter months. In the following spring he again left his native island with his worthy employer, Mr. Martin, in the ship *Occola*, for Milford. They had not been at sea more than ten days before

---

She was perfectly firm, and apparently indifferent to the rude gaze of the multitude. After praying with the clergyman—a Roman Catholic priest—the crucifix was placed upon her neck, and a white handkerchief in her hand. She was dressed in a long white robe, and her arms were bound behind her with a black cord.

Her body had become so light through grief and suffering, that when the platform fell she dangled in the air. Oh! it was painful—horrible to any who possessed the feelings of humanity, to witness such a spectacle. The struggles of the dying girl lasted several minutes before her spirit fled to a more just tribunal.

Merciful God! are such scenes to be continued in the face of a civilized world? Are such atrocious butcheries for ever to be permitted? To what hellish depravity does slavery debase the human mind! Here is a scene in which the principal municipal officers of the city of New Orleans—most of whom were fathers—are participating in an act of deliberate murder—one that can have no plea of justification beyond the laws framed by monsters, compared with whom Nero and Robespierre were merciful!—ED.

"The following additional example may be given of the contempt for the law exhibited in America:—A black man at St. Louis, in Missouri, named M'Intosh, who had stabbed an officer by whom he was arrested, was tied to a tree in the middle of the city by the inhabitants, was surrounded by piles of wood, and slowly burned to death. The details of the murder are dreadful.

"The honourable (?) Luke F. Lawless (not an inappropriate name), Judge of the Circuit Court of Missouri, decided officially that, "as the burning of M'Intosh was the act of a *majority*, it was a case that transcended the jurisdiction of the Grand Jury!"—*A Brief Notice of American Slavery.*

the yellow fever made its appearance among the passengers, six of whom came under its influence, among the number Benson's kind master and friend, who, with three others, were committed to the deep.

Few circumstances caused the grateful Benson more grief than the loss of this excellent man, who, had he lived, would, there can be little doubt, have purchased the freedom of Benson's poor old father, and have had him conveyed back to the partner of his bosom in Bermuda, as he frequently promised Benson he would do on his next return to America.

Benson arrived in safety in Milford Haven, in 1844. The ship *Occola* was next bound for Savannah, in the United States. This being a slave port, he feared if he returned he might be apprehended as a deserter. He therefore quitted the *Occola*, taking with him an excellent character, written by Captain Robertson, the commander. From Milford he walked to Swansea, and obtained employment at the establishment of Messrs. Bath and Grove, members of the Society of Friends, and stayed with them as long as they could find occupation for him. He next sailed in a schooner to Falmouth, where he worked in the mines belonging to Mr. Vivian, near Copperhouse, and continued in this employ until his health failed him. Having been accustomed to the glowing sun of the tropics, his being continually confined underground did not suit his constitution.

Since then he has found occasional employment as assistant-waiter in hotels and taverns. Among other situations, he mentions Mrs Richmond's, at the Bengal Arms, and Mr. Church's, at the Plough, Cheltenham, where he was treated with much kindness. Latterly he became so much reduced through sickness, as to be unable to undertake any laborious occupation. The writer met him in the streets at Worcester, procuring a scanty subsistence by the sale of religious tracts, and invited him to call at his residence, when he obtained this eventful history.

Benson accompanied the writer in his visits to several other towns, but at length left him with the intention of proceeding to Liverpool to procure a passage back to his native island of Bermuda. From all he saw of him he is induced to believe him honest and sincere.

Should this little work chance to meet the eye of Benjamin, the writer begs to assure him he will gladly share with him any profit that may arise from the sale.

INDEXES.

INDEX TO *OCEOLA NIKKANOCHEE*.

Aborigines, 72, 197
Aborigines' Protective Society, v–vi
Allachua, 203
Americans, 34, 38, 43
Appalachee Indians, 1, 2

Bailey, Major, 224, 226
Ball-play (game), 119
Bell, Captain, 65, 202, 203
Big Prairie, 77
Black Creek, 225
Black Point, 203

Call, Governor Richard Keith, 203
Camp King, 25
Catlin, George, 10, 23, 31, 146, 194, 195, 196
Charleston, S.C., 23, 39, 43, 201
Chattahoochee River, 1, 65
Cherokee Indians, 22
Choctawhatchee Bay, 225
Clinch, General Duncan L., 26, 29, 30, 32, 36
Coaeta River, 1
Conchatti, 128, 130

Coontee, 89
Creek Indians, 1, 22

Dade, Major Francis L., 5, 6, 34
Dexter, Horatio S., 65, 73, 202, 203
Donovan, phrenologist, 216, 217

East Florida Advocate, 203
Echa, 116
Econchatti, Mico, 63, 64, 65, 66, 78, 79, 86, 88, 92, 105, 115, 130, 158, 162, 202, 203, 217; meaning of, 65, 130, 131; mother of, 67, 68
Econfonee River, 227
Egyptian Hall, 23
Enamatkla, traitor, 32
Euchee tribe, 73, 74

Finholloway River, 227
Florida, East, 38, 56
Florida, governor of, 65, 81, 100, 129, 130, 141, 202, 219
Florida Paper, 223
Fort Andrews, 227, 228
Fort Drane, 35
Fort Frank-Brook, 227
Fort King, 223
Fort Moultrie, 43
Frelinghuysen, Senator, 219

Graham, Captain John, 49, 50, 52, 53, 54, 57, 58, 59, 60, 61, 129

Hall, Captain, 226, 228
Hernandez, General, 36, 37, 221
Highlanders, 51
Hitchcock, Captain, 35, 36
Holmes, Captain, 221, 222
Hukkasykee, 56
Hulwagus, 121

Indian Mary, 163, 164, 170, 171; husband of, 164, 165, 166, 167, 172; daughter of, 167, 168, 169, 171, 172, 173

INDEXES.

Indian names, 18
Iste-Chatti, 17

Jackson Trail, 227
Jacksonville, 100, 113, 123, 131
Jessup, General, 37, 201

King, Camp, 25

LaGrange, 225
Lawrence, 225

Mask dance, 119, 120, 121
Mason, Captain, 223
Micanopy, 203
Mikkasookies, 22
Missouri River, 136
Moultrie Creek, Treaty of, 160, 205-215
Muscogulgees, 1

Nathleocee, 49, 53, 54, 57, 60, 61
Nelson, Miss, 136
Newnansville, 97, 99, 101, 102, 110, 111, 112, 203
Nikkanochee, Oceola, 9, 19, 217; cast of head, 216, 217; Prince of Econchatti, 17, 19; protegee, vii, ix; orphan, ix; adoption of, ix; meaning of, 18
North American Indians, manners & customs, 10
Norton, Adjutant, 226

Oceola, 21, 23, 24, 28, 30, 32, 33, 35, 36, 37, 38, 39, 51, 52, 53, 59, 60, 64, 65, 68, 80, 81, 83, 86, 87, 90, 91, 92, 93, 94, 97, 104, 105, 109, 113; early days, 115, 118, 120, 123, 129, 130, 134, 174, 180, 186, 188, 189, 190, 192, 193, 201, 202, 220; chief, 20, 112, 219; uncle of Nikkanochee, 21
Ouithlacoochee, battle of, 33, 61

Pensacola Gazette, 225
Philip, King, capture of son, 221
Powell, 21

Reid, Judge Robert Raymond, 129

Reid, Mrs. Robert Raymond, 130
Regulus, 3
Riley, Colonel, 223
Rocky Mountains, 10

St. Augustine, 38, 49, 61, 62, 72, 79, 100, 129, 130, 171, 181, 182, 186, 202, 221
St. Augustine Herald, 221
St. Augustine News, 203, 223
St. Johns River, 6, 131, 132, 160, 163, 168, 180, 188, 192
Sanderson, Lieutenant, 203
Saufkee, 116
Scotland, 50
Seminole Indians, 1, 2, 6, 11, 20, 24, 28, 34, 37, 38, 43, 58, 73, 112, 175, 177; agent for, 65; amusements, 143, 144, 145, 146, 147, 148, 149, 150, 151, 152, 153; chieftain, 39; etiquette, 154, 155, 156; language, 130; medicine, 141, 142, 204, 219; nation, 58; religion, 157, 158; warriors' dirge, 41, 58
Seminole War, 49, 80
Shields, James, 102, 110, 113
Simmons, Dr. William Hayne, 130
Street, Alfred, 43
Suwannee River, 2

Tallahassee, 203
Tallahassee River, 2
Thomas's Old Mills, 227
Thompson, General Wiley, 27, 28, 29, 30, 32
Tomaka, 72
Townsend, Captain, 228

United States, 33, 38
United States Army, 65, 129
Uphetaikas (garments), 57

Warren, Colonel John, 97, 110, 111, 113, 123, 124
Washington Paper, 221
Washington Theatre, 136
Weedon, Dr., 201

INDEXES.

White, Joseph M., 204
Wilkin, Frank A., 74, 154

Yahchilanee and Allaha, 73–79
Yancton Indians, 137
Yemassee Indians, 1

INDEX TO *JANE JOHNS*.

Alachua, 9

Bigelow, Robert, 29
Black Creek, 16, 25, 26, 27
Blanchard, Captain H. R., 27, 29
Brandy-Branch, 27
Brown, Rev. David, 19, 18–22, 23
Brown's sermons, 18–22, 23

Charleston, 28

Dade, Francis L., 21
Dell, Colonel James, 9, 27, 29
Doggett, John L., 29
Dunlawton battle, 20, 21

East Florida, 7, 9, 28
Eubank, Mr., 10, 26

Faulk, John, 9

Gardiner, D. S., 29
Gould, death of, 21*n*

Hall, Mr. & Mrs., Jane Johns' parents, 8, 9, 16
Hall, Jane, 8, 9
Hart, Major, 10, 24, 29
Higginbotham, Mr., Indian attack on, 24
Hollingsworth, James, 7

Jacksonville, 9, 11, 12, 24, 28, 29

Jacksonville Courier, 12, 24–28
Johns, Clement, Jane's husband, 9, 10, 13, 16, 24, 25, 26
Johns, Jane: parents, 7–8; birth, 8; scalping of, 10–15, 24–28; discovered by father-in-law, 16; attended by Dr. Welch, 9–11; carried to Jacksonville, 12
Johns, Mr., Clement's father, 16, 26–27

Kingsley's Pond, 27

Lane, Mrs., 8
Lowder, Mr., 24, 26
Lowther, Mr., 16

McCormick, Mr., 24
McKinney, Mr., 26
Martinelly, Domingo, 20n
Miller, Frederick, 9
Mills, Colonel, 29

New River, 9

Payne's Prairie, 26
Pearson's Island, 8
Phillips, H. H., 29
Pierce, Major, 27
Pierson, John, 28
Pinckston, M. K., 29
Priest, Captain, 27
Priest, George, 9, 12
Priest, Granville, 9
Pritchard, Daniel, 7
Putnam, 21

Ratcliff, Mr., 26
Richards, Mr., 27
Rider, Emory, 29

St. Augustine, 7, 8, 23
St. John's River, 7, 8
St. Mary's River, 9

INDEXES. 7

Seminole Indians: attack the Halls' home, 7-8; attack the
  Johns' home, 10, 13-15, 25; kill Clement Johns, 10, 13,
  25; wound and scalp Jane Johns, 11, 13-15, 25;
  attack Higginbotham home, 24; escape, 26-27
Spanish Commandant, 7
Sparkman, Mr., 10, 25, 26
Sweet Water Branch, 8

Tallahassee Road, 24
Thigpen, Captain John L., 9, 10, 12, 28
Trout Creek, 7

Welch, Dr. Andrew: attends Mrs. Johns, 9-11; takes her
  to Jacksonville, 12; journal of, 9-12; offers services, 27;
  letter of Jacksonville citizens to, 28-29

INDEX TO *BENJAMIN BENSON*.

Africa, Benson's father in, 5, 11
America, 16, 34
Appalachicola, Fla., 21

Bath & Grove, Messrs., Benson's employers, 34
Belise, La., 24
Bengal Arms, the, Cheltenham, 34
Benson, Anthony, brother, 6-7, 19
Benson, Benjamin: parents, 5, 17-19, 21, 28, 33; brothers
  and sisters, 5-7, 19; birth, 8; childhood, 8-10; taken to
  U.S., 9-16; taken back to Bermuda, 15-19; freed by
  English law, 18-19; travels to U.S. & England, 19-24;
  in chain-gang in Louisiana, 24; sold back in slavery, 24;
  escapes, 25-27; returns to Bermuda, 28, 31; arrested in
  North Carolina, 31-32; in England, 32-35; meets Welch,
  35
Benson, George, brother, 5, 6
Benson, Judith, sister, 5
Benson, Robert, brother, 6
Benson, Sally, sister, 5, 7
Bermuda, 5, 6, 8, 16, 17, 19, 28, 31, 32, 33, 34, 35
Brighton, 33

Charleston Courier, 8n–9n
Cheltenham, 32, 35
Church, Mr., Benson's employer, 35
Clerical slaveowners, 28n–29n
Copperhouse, 34
Craft, Stephen, owner of Sally, 5

Davenport, Mr., owner of Benson's parents, 5
Davenport, Miss, owner of Anthony, 6
Douglass, Frederick, 22n–23n

Egbert, Benson sails on, 19
England, 22, 32, 33
English government, 17
English law frees slaves, 18–19
Escape from slavery: Benson's, 25–27; punishment for aiding, 27n

Falmouth, 34

Gambia, birthplace of Benson's father, 5
Georgia, Bensons in, 5

Halifax, 19

Jane, Benson sails on, 19, 21
Jubilee of Victory, 18

Liverpool, 22, 35
Long Island, N.Y., 5
Louisiana, 30

Margaret, slave girl, punishment of, 29–31
Martin, Mr., Benson's benefactor, 32, 33
Milford Haven, 33, 34
Milner, Mr., owner of Benson's father, 21
Mississippi River, 24
Mobile, Ala., 9, 10, 15, 21

Nassau, 26, 28
New Orleans, 11, 23, 24, 27

INDEXES.

New Providence, 26–27
New York, 5, 6, 19, 21, 33
Norie, Captain, 19
North Carolina, 6, 31–32

Occola, Benson sails on, 33, 34

Pamplico, Benson sails on, 31, 32
Pauline, slave girl, execution of, 31*n*–33*n*
Plough, the, Cheltenham, 35
Potter, Captain, 21

Race relations in U.S., 20–21
Raleigh Standard, 9*n*
Richmond, Mrs., Benson's employer, 35
Robertson, Captain, 34

S——, Mr., aids Benson's escape, 25–27
Savannah, 34
Slave life in U.S., descriptions of, 10–13, 24–25, 29–31
Slave ship, Benson on, 9–11, 16
Smith, Anthony's friend, 6
Smyth, Thomas, apology to Douglass, 22*n*–23*n*
Sneed, owner of Benson, 9
Society of Friends, 34
St. George's, Bermuda, Benson's birthplace, 8
St. Kitts, 16, 17
St. Mark's, Fla., 21
Swansea, 34

Tech, Mr., owner of Benson, 13–15
Terry, Louisiana slaveholder, 25*n*
Torry, Rev. Charles T., 27*n*
Trinidad, 6
Tripp, Robert's alias, 6
Trot, Thomas, owner of Benson, 16

United States, slave life in, 10–13, 24–25, 29–31

Vivian, Mr., Benson's employer, 34

INDEXES.

Washington, N.C., 13, 31
Welch, Dr. Andrew, meets Benson, 35
West Indies, 5, 16
William Goddard, Benson sails on, 21
Williams, John, Sally's husband, 5, 7
Wilmington, N.C., 6
Woodfork, buyer of Benson, 24, 28–30
Woodfork, Mrs., punishes Margaret, 29–31
Woodfork, George, victim of paralysis, 30
Worcester, 35

INDEX TO THE INTRODUCTION.

American Union, *xviii*
Apothecaries Hall, *xiv, xv, xxxiv–xxxv*
Australia, Nikkanochee goes to, *xxxix*

Benson, Benjamin, *xl, xli, xlii*
Bermuda, *xl*
Brockbank, William, *xli*
Brown, the Reverend Mr., *xlii*
Catlin, George, paints Nikkanochee's portrait, *xxxvi*
Charleston, S.C., *xxiii, xxiv, xxv, xxvi, xxvii, xxxv, xli*
Chipping Onger, *xv*
Clark, Frances Ann, Welch's second wife, *xvi, xvii*

Dade, Major Francis L., *xxv, xliii*
Dell, Colonel James, *xlii*
Donovan, phrenologist, *xxxvi–xxxvii*
Donovan, H. C., *xxxvii*
Douvilles, Mrs., *xxiv*

Egyptian Hall, Nikkanochee visits, *xxxvi*
Exit, *xxvi*

Florida, *xvi, xvii, xviii, xxiii, xxv, xxvi, xxvii, xxxiii, xxxiv*
Florida Militia, *xxii*
Fort Sumter, *xxv, xxxv*

Georgia, *xviii*
Gliddon, Jane, Welch's first wife, *xv*, *xvi*
Gould, James, St. Augustine editor, *xvii*, *xix*, *xx*, *xxiii*
Green, R & H, Nikkanochee apprenticed to, *xxxix*

Jacksonville, Fla., *xvii*, *xx*, *xxi*, *xxii*, *xxiii*, *xxiv*, *xxvi*, *xxviii*, *xxix*
Jacksonville Courier, *xxi*
Johns, Jane: scalping of, *xx*, *xxi*, *xxii*; recovery, *xxiii*, *xxiv*; attended by Dr. Welch, *xxv*, *xxvii*, *xli*; dedication of narrative, *xxv*, *xlii*
Jones, John Dalston, Welch's partner, *xl*

Kingsland Road, *xiv*, *xxxiv*

Lake Okeechobee, *xix*
Liverpool, England, *xxxiv*
London Phrenological Institute, *xxxvi*

Mansion House, Savannah, *xxiv*, *xxv*
Middlesex County, *xiv–xv*
Mill Hill Grammar School, Nikkanochee attends, *xxxviii–xxxix*
Moultrie Creek, Treaty of, *xix*

Narrative of the Early Days and Remembrances of Oceola Nikkanochee, A, *xiv*, *xlii*, *xliii*
Narrative of the Life of Benjamin Benson, A, *xiv*, *xv*, *xlii*
Narrative of the Life and Sufferings of Mrs. Jane Johns, A, *xiv*, *xxi*, *xxxv*, *xlii*
Nassau, *xli*
Nazeing, Welch's birthplace, *xiv*, *xv*
Neufville, the Reverend Edward, *xxiv*
Nikkanochee, Oceola: brought as war captive to Jacksonville by Colonel Warren, *xxii*, *xxvi*; lives with the Warren family, *xxii*, *xxvi–xxvii*; his effect on Welch, *xxii–xxiii*, *xxvi–xxvii*; adopted by Welch, *xxvii*; lives with Welch at St. Johns in Florida, *xxviii–xxxiii*; carried by Welch to England, *xxxiii–xxxiv*; his portrait by George Catlin, *xxxvi*; his portrait by Frank A. Wilkin, *xxxvi*; his head cast by the phrenologist Donovan, *xxxvi–xxxvii*; adopted

by the Sherman family, *xxxvii–xxxviii*; attends Mill Hill Grammar School, *xxxviii–xxxix*; apprenticed as a seaman, *xxxix*; becomes first mate, *xxxix*; goes to Australia, *xxxix*; passes from view, *xxxix*

Pulaski House, Savannah, *xxiv*

Royal Academy, *xxxvi*
Royal College of Surgeons, *xiv, xxxiv*

St. Augustine, *xvii, xxx*
St. John-at-Hackney, *xliii*
St. Johns, Welch's Florida home, *xxvi, xxviii, xxx–xxxiii*
St. Johns County Court, *xvii*
St. Johns River, *xix, xxvi, xxix*
St. Leonard Parish, *xiv, xxxiv*
Savannah, Ga., *xxiii, xxv, xxvi, xxxiv, xxxv*
Savannah Daily Georgian, *xxiv*
Seminole Indians: Welch's attitude toward, *xvii–xviii, xx–xxiii, xxvi–xxviii, xlii–xliii*; and Florida settlers, *xviii–xix*; Treaty of Moultrie Creek, *xix*; scalp Jane Johns, *xx*; Nikkanochee a son of, *xxii*; and the Dade Massacre, *xxv*
Severn River, *xl*
Sherman, the Reverend James, and family, adopt Nikkanochee, *xxxvii–xxxix*
Shoreditch, *xv*
Slavery, Welch's attitude toward, *xxx–xxxii, xl–xliii*
Slaves, hired by Welch, *xxx–xxxii*
Smith, General Peter Sken, *xxxii*

Trafalgar Square, *xxxvi*
Treatise on Tinea Capitis, *xxxiv–xxxv*

Warren, Colonel John, *xxii, xxvi, xxvii*
Welch, Emily, daughter, *xv*
Welch, Frances Ann Clark, second wife, *xvi, xvii*
Welch, Gesborne Henry, nephew, *xvii*
Welch, Henry James Wordsworth, son, *xv, xl*
Welch, James Andrew: his birth, *xiv*; his life, *xiv, xv, xlii–xliii*; his children, *xv–xvi*; his travels, *xvi, xvii, xix*;

attends Jane Johns, *xx–xxv, xxvii*; and Nikkanochee,
xxii–xxiii, xxvi–xxxiv, xxxvi–xxxviii, xlii–xliii
Welch, Jane, daughter, *xv*
Welch, Jane Gliddon, first wife, *xv, xvi*
Welch, William and Mary, parents, *xiv*
West Indies, *xvi*
Wilkin, Frank A., Nikkanochee's portrait by, *xxxvi*
Worcester, *xl, xli*

www.ingramcontent.com/pod-product-compliance
Lightning Source LLC
Chambersburg PA
CBHW021847230426
43671CB00006B/302